本教材获海南热带海洋学院教材基金资助

2014年三亚市院地科技合作项目（外语学习者计算机网络生态环境构建与优化研究2014YD19）

On Optimizing the Cyber-based Ecological
Environment for Foreign Language Learners

外语学习者计算机网络生态环境优化研究

魏　晶　著

U0736403

中国海洋大学出版社

·青岛·

图书在版编目（CIP）数据

外语学习者计算机网络生态环境优化研究：英文 /
魏晶著. —青岛：中国海洋大学出版社, 2017.11
　　ISBN 978-7-5670-1631-6

　　Ⅰ.①外⋯　Ⅱ.①魏⋯　Ⅲ.①英语—网络教学—教学
研究—英文　Ⅳ.①H319.3

　　中国版本图书馆CIP数据核字（2017）第283945号

外语学习者计算机网络生态环境优化研究

出版发行	中国海洋大学出版社
社　　址	青岛市香港东路23号　　　邮政编码　266071
网　　址	http://www.ouc-press.com
出 版 人	杨立敏
责任编辑	吴欣欣
电　　话	0532-85901092
电子信箱	wuxinxin0532@126.com
印　　制	日照报业印刷有限公司
版　　次	2018年3月第1版
印　　次	2018年3月第1次印刷
成品尺寸	185 mm × 260 mm
印　　张	10.5
字　　数	230千
印　　数	1-1000
定　　价	27.00元
订购电话	0532-82032573（传真）

发现印装质量问题，请致电0633-8221365，由印刷厂负责调换。

PREFACE

From the 1990s onwards, modern information technology, taking computer networks as the core, is developing rapidly. In 2004, "College English Curriculum Requirements（For Trial Implementation）" was issued by the Ministry of Education, China, proposing "Computer-and-Classroom-Based English Teaching Mode". The new teaching reform is to improve the traditional English teaching mode and build the network-based autonomous foreign language learning mode by establishing three-dimensional network-based multimedia teaching system. Thus the position of computer networks is defined as an indispensable part of foreign language teaching, to be brought up for the first time in the history of foreign language education. Computer networks are for the first time taken seriously and from then on the integration of computer networks into foreign language curriculum truly began.

As the computer networks technology and foreign language teaching belong to two different disciplines, the integration of computer networks into foreign language curriculum will inevitably lead to the changes of traditional teaching factors, such as its teaching model, teaching objectives, methods, tools, materials, curriculum and others. The changes of these factors correspondingly bring about the changes of teaching concepts. Obviously, these changes have broken the balance of foreign language learners' traditional ecological environment. The imbalanced learning environment will undoubtedly witness the occurrence of many disorders. Interdisciplinary integration is a tendency of the scientific development in the 21st century. Therefore, it is necessary to adopt a perspective of constructing a new learning environment to reexamine foreign language learning under the frame of ecology, the principles of which can offer feasible solutions to the imbalanced problems. It aims to construct and optimize foreign language learners' ecological environment under the background of computer networks, by making it into a new ecological balance featured with the harmonious, dynamic, flexible and healthy development.

With this targeting task, the following main problems need to be combed and solved. In what way does computer networks technology affect foreign language learning? What is the intrinsic relationship between computer networks technology and foreign language learning? What kinds of imbalances are brought about by the integration of computer networks into foreign language curriculum? What are the causes for these disorders? How to remove these disorders? Why is it necessary to construct the new ecological environment for learners under the background of computer networks technology? How to optimize this imbalanced ecological learning environment to achieve the new ecological balance among various factors? What are the conditions and requirements to construct a balanced ecological learning environment? It is quite obvious that exploring the solutions to these issues can promote the depth of current theoretical research of cyber-based foreign language learning environment in China, making the complicated theoretical exploration of interdisciplinary research more refined, systematic and perfect. This study will not only for the first time enrich and perfect the theoretical system of constructing foreign language environment under the background of computer networks, but also make up for the blank in the study of constructing and optimizing learning environment. More importantly, this study will promote the construction of an ecological learning model as well as the development of college foreign language teaching.

This study, based on the proposition and reflection, as well as the exploration and solution to the above problems, mainly targets at the following research topic. The computer-network-based foreign language learning has become the auxiliary practice and preferential choice for foreign language study in current colleges and universities, thus based on ecological theories, by exploring and analyzing cyber-based foreign language environment as well as by relating to its empirical study and field investigation, this study attempts to put forward the fundamental principles and requirements for optimizing cyber-based foreign language learning environment into an integrated, dynamic and balanced ecological environment.

The main arguments in this study can be summarized into the following two aspects:

Firstly, the integration of computer networks into foreign language teaching and learning has changed the traditional way of information transmission and acceptance. Besides, the integration form of teaching content and teaching activities has taken drastic changes. The teaching concepts and teaching values as well as teaching evaluation standards have changed a great deal. These changes have broken the balance of traditional teaching environment. Correspondingly, the imbalance of teaching environment has led to the imbalance of students' learning environment. Therefore, this study is conducted to achieve its ecological balance again by optimizing cyber-based foreign language learning environment with ecological principles and ideologies.

Secondly, the ecological niche theory and the theory of ecological balance are especially used to optimize four imbalanced sub-ecological environments. The fundamental requirements and principles for its optimization have been proposed. Four optimized ecological environments can essentially realize the informationization of foreign language. That is to say, on the one hand, the information technologies can be maximumly integrated into foreign language curricula to achieve the real application of computer networks into students' learning and teachers' teaching; on the other hand, the information technologies are reflected by foreign language learning curricula by cultivating students' interest in foreign language study and their language sense so that the students can readily handle all the problems in an informationized way during the process of foreign language learning. Four sub-ecological environments are of interdependence, interaction, mutual adaptation, and coordinative unification, constituting a wholly dynamic and balanced foreign language learners' ecological environment.

The research methods adopted in the paper are literature review and statistical analysis. With this macro research, some other quantitative studies are also employed, such as questionnaires and case study, aiming to prove the appropriateness and preciseness of some microscopic views and basic structures.

The structure for its argumentation is mainly divided into seven chapters:

The first chapter, presentation of the problems. Through an analysis of the relationship between computer technologies and foreign language teaching as well as its integration mechanism, this chapter mainly proposes the imbalances of four sub-ecological environments due to the integration of computer networks into foreign language curriculum, which shows that the original ecological learning environment has disequilibrated after the integration. Four imbalanced sub-ecological environments refer to physical learning environment, resourceful learning environment, technological learning environment and emotional learning environment.

The second chapter, literature review and theoretic framework. By making full use of and combing through all research literatures on cyber-based foreign language learners' ecological environment at home and abroad, the author intends to seek for the theoretical basis for constructing and optimizing cyber-based foreign language learners' ecological environment by relying on the theory of Computer-Assisted Language Learning, the relevance between multimedia networks and information technologies and foreign language learning, as well as the Cognitivism (learning theory) , Constructivism (learning theory) and the theory of Ecology. In addition, the article has dug out all relevant research tracks through literature reviews and made full use of the existing research results to provide support and foundation for this study.

The third chapter, overview on the imbalance problems of cyber-based foreign language learners' ecological environment. The author points out the causes of imbalances of physical learning environment, resourceful learning environment, technological learning environment and emotional learning environment. Four learning environments are seriously imbalanced. The learning modes, concepts, learning methods, learning content, learning media, etc. are incompatible with existing cyber-based learning conditions, faculty force, students, management quality and supporting teaching materials; learners' social environment, regulatory mechanism, management level, emotional and psychological factors, etc. are all more or less in disorder. These imbalances or disorders undoubtedly have brought about an unbalanced informationized learning environment, which is impossible to survive in the school education system.

The fourth chapter, the assumption to solve problems. With ecological niche and ecosystem balance theories to optimize the imbalanced four learning environments, this chapter puts forward the fundamental requirements and principles of optimization, to deduce the model of network-based ecological learning and the model of cyber-based ecological environments for foreign language learning. Through optimization, learners, teachers, computers and learning contents are no longer in one-way relation. Instead, they are in two-way mutual connection, interaction, interdependence and mutual conversion. The students have consequently become the active knowledge builder. The cyber-based foreign language learners' ecological environment, after optimization, can not only reflect ecological laws and principles, but also be a kind of student-centered integration of all ecological factors, with the features of being manipulated, perfected, optimized and developed, casting a positive influence on learners.

The fifth chapter, the supporting arguments and proofs for the necessity of optimizing the imbalanced cyber-based ecological environment for foreign language learners by adopting the methods of quantitative analysis and the experimental study. The main research objective in this paper is to explore, summarize and validate the theory of constructing and optimizing the cyber-based ecological environment for foreign language learners by two double-decks—theory and practice, and to prove the necessity of achieving a new balance of the ecological environment.

The experimental section is presented in this chapter. Five teachers from Qiongzhou University have conducted a series of experiments for the whole semester. 300 students were randomly chosen to do 11 kinds of questionnaires, informal discussions and English tests, involving their experiences or viewpoints on four sub-ecological environments（namely physical learning environment, resourceful learning environment, technological learning environment and emotional learning environment）, their actual use of computer networks in college English class, their perspective of teachers' role, students' role, and the positioning of computers in learning, and their present attitudes for college students' autonomous English learning under the environment of computer networks. With all of these, college students' actual needs are handy and their opinions or suggestions are collected. This kind of analysis is to provide relevant empirical basis for building and optimizing the model of cyber-based foreign language learners' ecological environment.

The sixth chapter, summary. By making comparisons between the cyber-based ecological learning environment to be optimized and the one already optimized, it is quite obvious that the optimized learning environment is generally stepping towards balanced development. The optimized learning environment is an ecological system with balanced input and output of material flow, information flow, energy flow and emotion flow. The optimized and balanced learning environment under the background of computer networks can be interpreted from three levels—macro-ecology, meso-ecology and micro-ecology. The ecological balance of macro-ecology displays the balance between four sub-environments which are material learning environment, resourceful learning environment, technological learning environment and emotional learning environment under the background of computer networks. The ecological balance of meso-ecology is viewed from the balance between various elements within the learning ecological environment. And the ecological balance of micro-ecology refers to the balance between internal factors in each sub-environment. The cyber-based ecological environment for foreign language learners is a big integrated system which covers all sides and aspects of each sub-environment. Moreover, each sub-environment forms a new ecological system respectively. Within each independent sub-environment and system, various factors interact with each other through mutual adaptation, finally promoting the dynamic balance of the entire system in turn. The result of examining and optimizing cyber-based learning ecological environment from the ecological perspective is that whether it is an individual ecological niche like student, teacher, teaching administrator and technical staff or it is the group niche like group of students and group of teachers, all ecological factors are playing their respective roles in their respective niches. In other words, all ecological factors are in the appropriate and dynamic niches. Under the cyber-based ecological environment for learners, four sub-environments rely on each other, restricting each other and finally coming to an integrated unity through the process of balance—imbalance—a new balance.

Through the above systematic discussions, it comes to a conclusion that based on Computer-Assisted Language Learning theory, the Cognitivism, Constructivism and Ecology theory, the cyber-based ecological environment for foreign language learners, from inductive reasoning to conducting empirical study, then to the construction of the model, has been theoretically created, which is characterized by systematic integrity, stable balance as well as dynamic openness.

Finally, the seventh chapter, some innovations and limitations of the study are pointed out and discussed. Some prospects for future studies have also been made.

CONTENTS

1.1

The Origin of the Topic Selection

1.1.1 Background

Since the integration of computer network technologies into college students' life and study, college students' way of life and way of study have undergone profound changes. The convenient and intelligent electronic equipments are becoming their daily entertainment, communication or learning tools without which they can hardly survive. Their life, communication, study, and entertainment, even their language, behavior, thoughts, character, etc. are all deeply influenced or molded by network culture. In the face of such a generation as a teaching object group, the college foreign language teaching, including foreign language teachers, teaching materials, teaching methods and other elements, must be precisely positioned, either to get adapted or to be eliminated. China's foreign language teaching, generally speaking, is to improve the efficiency in its own development, to adapt to the social changes and conform to the development of technology. First and foremost, the teaching concept and teaching method must be changed. This hinges on the enhancement of teachers' informational technology literacy, the updating of the teaching mode which signifies the transfer from the original teaching type of "textbook, blackboard, chalk and teachers' monologues" into the network-based and informationized style. Changing the way of technology does not mean the renewal or replacement of teaching means, equipments and abilities, but an all-round adaptation of consciousness, cultures and ways of thinking, which is a must for current college foreign language teachers and foreign language teaching researches.

The integration of computer networks into foreign language teaching and learning has changed the traditional way of information transmission and acceptance. Besides, the integration form of teaching content and teaching activities has taken drastic changes. The teaching concept and teaching values as well as its evaluation standards have changed a great deal. These changes have broken the balance of traditional teaching environment. The imbalances of teaching environment are characterized by the following five aspects: inconformity between national education policies and the actual implementations in local schools; inconsistency between concept and practice; imbalance between technology and its application; inadaptation between new teaching mode and traditional teaching system; disorders between teaching process and teaching organization or management. What's more, the imbalance of teaching environment causes many disorders in students' learning environment. The application of information technology in foreign language education has a great effect on the construction of foreign language learners' cyber-based learning environment and also on foreign language learners' development. However, the current cyber-based learning environment is full of disorders and imbalances, not an ideal virtual environment.

1.1.2 Research Basis and Conditions

The research of foreign language teaching and network technology is actually not a new topic to researchers and scholars. Apart from the numerous academic articles and dissertations, it is also natural for some scholars to conduct their explorations on foreign language teaching techniques （including computers, networks, multimedia foreign language teaching and other various concepts） from their professional accumulation and teaching experience. They are earnestly engaged in detailed research of teaching practices for informationized foreign language teaching and tenaciously reflect on the modernization of foreign language teaching.

It would be safe to say that from the new period onwards those scholars have been on their way to the research exploration of foreign language teaching. The new century has especially witnessed fruitful productions. With the rapid development of educational technologies since the new century onward and the absorption of the essence of its technology-based teaching theory as well as the research results on disciplinary teaching, another batch of outstanding research works are produced in the field of foreign language teaching. The representative works are as follows:

Educational Technology and Foreign Language Teaching（Dai Zhengnan & Huang Guangyuan, 1998）, *Modern Educational Technology and Modern Foreign Language Teaching*（He Gaoda, 2002）, *The Application of Computers in English Education*（Chen Hong & Liu Beili, 2005）, *Computers and English Teaching—from Theory to Practice*（Gu Yueguo, 2006）, *Computer-Assisted Language Learning—Theory and Practice*（Jia Guodong, 2007）,

Computer-Assisted Second Language Research Methodology and Its Application（Wang Lifei, 2007）, *Information Technology and Foreign Language Teaching*（Liu Risheng, et al., 2007）, *Foreign Language Teaching Technology*（Cheng Dongyuan, 2008）, *The Theory of Modern Linguistics and Multimedia Foreign Language Teaching*（Zeng Fangben, 2010）, *A Practical Coursebook of Modern Education Technology and Foreign Language Teaching*（Wen Heping, et al., 2010）, *The Integration of Computers and Networks into Foreign Language Curriculum*（Chen Jianlin, 2010）, *The Research of Information Technology and Foreign Language Teaching—Theoretical Construction and Practical Exploration*（Chen Jianlin & Hu Jiasheng, 2010）, and other relevant works authorized by Gu Peiya（2006）, Wang Qi（2006）, Zhang Hongling（2010）, etc.

Besides the works mentioned above, research fruits including the development of abundant network-based or multimedia-based college English textbooks, the establishment of large and medium-sized corpus, the technological development of various computer-based and cyber-based examinations for college English students, English majors and non-English majors, etc.

Having engaged in foreign language teaching and research for quite many years, the author has always been taking the theoretical and practical integration and application of computer networks as well as information technologies into foreign language learning as the core, analyzing the various imbalances during the integration process and creating an optimization mode which can conduct to change the disorders and to achieve a balanced development of learning environment and the enhancement of foreign language teaching.

All of the above are origins for this study.

1.2

The Targeting Problems

In light of the mentioned items, this study attempts to take the following concerns into account:

1）In a time of the spreading information technology, what impact does information technology represented by computer networks have on foreign language teaching? What is the fundamental relationship between computer technology and foreign language teaching?

2）What kinds of imbalances of environment during the integration of computer networks into foreign language curriculum are? What are the causes for these imbalances? How to eliminate them?

3）Why is it necessary to construct the new ecological environment for learners under the background of multimedia and network technologies? What are the basic requirements and principles of this ecological environment? How to optimize this imbalanced ecological learning environment to achieve the new ecological balance among various factors?

It is quite obvious that exploring the solutions to these issues can make an induction from the current theoretical research of cyber-based foreign language learning environment in China, make the complicated theoretical exploration of interdisciplinary research more refined, systematic and perfect. This study will not only for the first time enrich and perfect the theoretical system of constructing foreign language environment under the background of multimedia and networks, as well as make up for the blank in the study of constructing and optimizing learning environment. More importantly, this study will promote the construction of an ecological teaching model as well as the development of college foreign language teaching.

1.3
Research Purpose and Significance

The construction of cyber-based learning environment followed by the application of information technology in English education has become an important factor in students' learning. However, due to the existing problems in the construction of environment and maintenance operation, etc., there is low efficiency in the web environment and web-based course, online community, etc., followed by students' learning problems in resource utilization, emotional exchanges and so on. That is to say, the environment is seriously imbalanced. Therefore, it is of necessity to construct a dynamic, harmonious and ecological computer-network-based learning system and environment with sustainable momentum and development from a new point of view, which will constitute another influential research project for theoretical and practical studies on current computer-based foreign language education.

The development of ecology has provided a new perspective for many research projects. From the ecological perspective, the dissertation targets at using the basic principles of ecology to optimize computer-network-based foreign language learning environment in order to achieve ecological balance again. The present study will undoubtedly put energy into the study of CALL （Computer-assisted Language Learning） and certainly deepen the research subject of "integrating information technology of networks into foreign language curriculum". It is also a necessary step to achieve the objectives of college English teaching reform and crucial to consolidating the research foundations for teaching mode, curriculum positioning, student orientation, teacher's role and evaluation system under the cyber-based environment.

In the dissertation, it is to provide practical solutions to the imbalances in current computer-network-based foreign language learning environment by optimizing the imbalanced learning environment according to ecological principles. The optimization can guarantee cyber-based learning efficiency and students' healthy and sustainable development. Through the analysis of topic-related questionnaire and SPSS, learners can clearly understand what the existing imbalances in computer-network-based foreign language learning environment are, and how to construct and optimize their "second learning virtual space". If foreign language learners, as the main ecological body in cyber-based ecological learning system, know what to do to create a good learning environment and get better involved in effective learning, it will cast a profound influence on maintaining beneficial circulation of computer-network-based ecological learning system.

1.4

Theoretical Background

A clear interdisciplinary theoretical structure is of necessity to construct and optimize cyber-based foreign language learners' ecological environment. The theoretical systems within this discipline cover such disciplines as pedagogy, education technology, mass communication, psychology, language teaching, language learning, sociology, information technology and other natural sciences and humanities. Therefore, the study has theoretical foundations of behaviorism, cognitivism, constructivism, ecology, etc. These postmodern thoughts with social, cultural and technological perspectives are gradually diluting their differences and integrated, finally into an ecologically integrated concept and mode featured by postmodernism, which serves as the theoretical pillar for the research of constructing and optimizing cyber-based ecological environment for foreign language learners.

◆ 1.5 ◆

Research Methods

The current study is based on the constructing foreign language learners' ecological environment under the background of network technologies, which decides the main methods of theoretical researches. In other words, under the frame of certain theories, theoretical demonstrations are deduced by network technology, foreign language teaching, constructivism, ecology, etc., in order to create a mode of constructing and optimizing the ecological environment for foreign language learners. On this macro level, other qualitative and quantitative research methods like literature review, statistical analysis are also adopted just to prove the appropriateness and preciseness of the mode. The concrete demonstrations are on two levels: macro-level—logical reasoning on theoretical level, micro-level—the level of teaching practice and mode construction.

First of all, with the reasoning of "network technology and foreign language teaching", by the analysis of multimedia network technology as well as foreign language teaching research data and the critical evaluation of the overall literature review, the study tries to draw the following conclusion: the integration of network technology into foreign language teaching has resulted in the changes of students' learning environment and the imbalances in different degrees.

Secondly, constructivism and ecology serve as the theoretical perspectives for optimizing the integrated environment of network technology and foreign language learning. Moreover, on the basis of literature review, fundamental principles and requirements for its environmental optimization are proposed to construct optimization mode. In other words, the research methods such as literature review and statistical analysis, etc., taking "network technology" as the breakthrough point, are used for the research of ecological environment, which helps to reach the dynamic balance within the mode of optimized ecological learning environment.

The demonstration process on these two levels cannot be separated apart with striking distinctions but an entirety interrelated intrinsically and harmoniously. The fulfillment of its theme structure requires a macro perspective. However, the study of specific patterns or modes requires both qualitative and quantitative research methods of all kinds, including not only objective methods like literature review, statistical analysis, etc., but also critical analysis of fact-based materials and representative viewpoints.

1.6

Structure and Main Content

The main arguments in this study can be summarized into the following aspects:

The first chapter, the integration of computer networks into foreign language teaching and learning has changed the traditional way of information transmission and acceptance. Besides, the integration form of teaching content and teaching activities has taken drastic changes. The teaching concept and teaching values as well as its evaluation standards have changed a great deal. These changes have broken the balance of traditional teaching environment. Correspondingly, the imbalance of teaching environment has led to the imbalance of students' learning environment. The students' learning environment is divided into four sub-ecological environments. The four sub-ecological environments refer to physical learning environment, resourceful learning environment, technological learning environment and emotional learning environment. Therefore, this study is conducted to re-achieve its ecological balance by optimizing cyber-based foreign language learning environment with ecological principles and ideologies.

The second chapter, literature review and theoretic framework. By making full use of and combing through all research literatures on cyber-based foreign language learners' ecological environment at home and abroad, the author intends to seek for the theoretical basis for constructing and optimizing cyber-based foreign language learners' ecological environment by relying on the theory of CALL, the relevance between multimedia network and information technologies and foreign language learning, as well as the Cognitivism (learning theory), Constructivism (learning theory) and the theory of Ecology. In addition, the article has dug out all relevant research tracks through literature reviews and made full use of the existing research results to provide support and foundation for this study.

The third chapter, overview of the imbalanced problems of cyber-based foreign language learners' ecological environment. The author points out the causes of imbalances of physical learning environment, resourceful learning environment, technological learning environment and emotional learning environment. Four learning environments are seriously imbalanced which can be concluded as follows: the learning modes, concepts, learning methods, learning content, learning media, etc. are incompatible with existing cyber-based learning conditions, faculty force, students, management quality and supporting teaching materials; learners' social environment, regulatory mechanism, management level, emotional and psychological factors, etc. are all more or less in disorder. These imbalances or disorders undoubtedly have brought about an unbalanced informationization learning environment, which is impossible to survive in the school education system.

The fourth chapter, the assumption of solving problems. With ecological niche and ecosystem balance theories to optimize the imbalanced four learning environments, this chapter puts forward the fundamental requirements and principles of optimization, to deduce the model of network-based ecological learning and the model of cyber-based ecological environments for foreign language learning. Through optimization, learners, teachers, computers and learning contents are no longer in one-way relation. Instead, they are in two-way mutual connection, interaction, interdependence and mutual conversion. The students have consequently become the active knowledge builder. The cyber-based foreign language learners' ecological environment, after optimization, can not only reflect ecological laws and principles, but also be a kind of student-centered integration of all ecological factors, with the features of being manipulated, perfected, optimized and developed, casting a positive influence on learners.

The fifth chapter, the supporting arguments and proofs for the necessity of optimizing the imbalanced cyber-based ecological environment for foreign language learners by adopting the methods of quantitative analysis and the experimental study. The main research object in this paper is to explore, summarize and validate the theory of constructing and optimizing the cyber-based ecological environment for foreign language learners by two double-decks: theory and practice, and to prove the necessity of achieving a new balance of the ecological environment.

It is about the experimental section. Five teachers from Qiongzhou University have conducted a series of experiments for the whole semester. 300 students were randomly chosen to do eleven kinds of questionnaires, informal discussions and English tests, involving their experiences or viewpoints on four sub-ecological environments（namely physical learning environment, resourceful learning environment, technological learning environment and emotional learning environment）, their actual use of computer networks in college English class, their perspective of teachers' role, students' role, and the positioning of computers in learning, and the present attitudes for college students' autonomous English learning under the environment of computer networks. With all of these, college students' actual needs are handy and their opinions or suggestions are collected. This kind of analysis is to provide relevant empirical basis for building and optimizing the model of cyber-based foreign language learners' ecological environment.

The sixth chapter, summary. To sum up, by making comparison between the cyber-based ecological learning environment to be optimized and the one already optimized, it is quite obvious that the optimized learning environment is generally stepping towards balanced development. The optimized learning environment is an ecological system with balanced input and output of material flow, information flow, energy flow and emotion flow. The optimized and balanced learning environment under the background of computer networks can be interpreted from three levels: macro-ecology, meso-ecology（mesoscopic-ecology） and micro-ecology. The ecological balance of macro-ecology displays the balance between four sub-environments which are material learning environment, resourceful learning environment, technological learning environment and emotional learning environment under the background of computer networks. The ecological balance of meso-ecology is viewed from the balance between various elements within the learning ecological environment. And the ecological balance of micro-ecology refers to the balance between internal factors in each sub-environment. The cyber-based ecological environment for foreign language learners itself is a big integrated system which covers all sides and aspects of each sub-environment. Moreover, each sub-environment forms a new ecological system respectively. Within each independent sub-environment and system, various factors interact with each other through mutual adaptation, finally promoting the dynamic balance of the entire system in turn. The result of examining and optimizing cyber-based learning ecological environment from ecological perspective is that whether it is an individual ecological niche like student, teacher, teaching administrator and technical staff or it is the group niche like group of students and group of teachers, all ecological factors are playing their respective roles in their respective niches. In other words, all ecological factors are in the appropriate and dynamic niches. Under the cyber-based ecological environment for learners, four sub-environments rely on each other, restricting each other and finally coming to an integrated unity through the process of balance—imbalance— a new balance.

Through the above systematic discussions, it comes to a conclusion that based on Computer-Assisted Language Learning theory, the Cognitivism, Constructivism and Ecology theory, the cyber-based ecological environment for foreign language learners, from inductive reasoning to conducting empirical study, then to the construction of the model, has theoretically created, which is characterized by systematic integrity, stable balance as well as dynamic openness.

Finally, the seventh chapter, some innovations and limitations of the study are pointed out and discussed. Some prospects for future studies are also made.

2 Chapter

Literature Review and Theoretical Framework

◆ **2.1** ◆

Literature Review

According to targeting topic requirements, centering around the theme of constructing and optimizing cyber-based ecological environment for foreign Language learners, the author, enclosing the two research lines of CALL and the present research status of ecological foreign language teaching and ecological environment for foreign language learners under the background of computer networks in the study, has collected and reviewed a large amount of literature materials. After combing through and defining all relevant literatures, the two lines are flowing into one theoretical primary line for the upcoming demonstration.

2.1.1 Previous Study of CALL Abroad and at Home

2.1.1.1 Previous Study of CALL Abroad

The study of CALL can be traced back to the 1960s. According to the division of Warschauer（1996）, the development of CALL has undergone three stages, namely the behavioral phase（behavioristic）, communicative stage（communicative）and current integrated stage（integrative）. In the 1990s, the world CALL was budding because of the rapid popularity of personal computers and the constant changes of network and multimedia technologies.

World CALL was actually a loose academic organization founded in 1998. Its member associations, in theory, should include "European Computer-Assisted Language Learning Association（EUROCALL）, American Computer-Assisted Language Learning Association（CALICO）, International Language Learning and Technology Association based in the

United States （IALLT）, Association of British University Language Center （AULC）, European Language Council （ELC）, Japanese Language Education and Technology Association （LET）, Union of European Higher Education Language Center （CERCLES）, Canadian Computer-Assisted Auxiliary Language Learning Association （CCALL/CELAO）, Australia Technology of Language Learning Association （ATELL）. And other associations closely related to CALL include Asia-Pacific Computer-Assisted Auxiliary Language Learning Association （APACALL）, Computer-Assisted Language Learning Association in south Korea （Asia CALL, Korea）, Computer-Assisted Language Learning Association in India （India CALL）, and the Pacific Computer-Assisted Language Learning Association （PACCALL）, etc. This shows World CALL covers a wide range of areas and scopes.

Associations and organizations of CALL all over the world will organize international CALL conferences or seminars regularly. Their own website, publications and academic journals, etc. are also on the regular agenda. Every year, many research articles on CALL are published, with representative papers compiled into collected papers. Apart from that, there have been many professional research journals on international computer-assisted language learning, such as ALSIC, SYSTEM, Athelstan Newsletter （TELL Digest）, CALICO: CALL, CALL-EJ, ALL Review, IJCALLT, IALLT: LLT, ON-CALL, ReCALL, and also CAFLE, the Chinese CALL Journal. The practical software of CALL developed by researchers is too numerous to be listed.

But throughout the recent decades of research work in the field of international CALL, we can clearly see that CALL turns out to be a very concrete as well as a broad concept. Its concreteness lies in the summary of CALL made by international fields of computer-assisted language learning, which focuses on the specific application of technology, that is, concerning the concrete process of the computer assisted language learning. For example, in August 2008 in Fukuoka, Japan, the third world seminar of computer-assisted language learning （World CALL 2008） had received 145 papers for theme speeches （see Table 2.1）. The subject matter involved nine aspects like teaching reform of CALL, computers functioning as the medium of communication, the design and development of teaching courseware, the application of new technologies, multimedia applications, corpus applications, online learning, the study of students and teachers, all of which were about the actual teaching problems.

Table 2.1: Statistical analysis of theme-based papers （Mo Jinguo, 2009:04）

Topics for Discussion	Quantity	Ratio
Teaching Reform of CALL	25	17.20%
Computers Mediated-Communication （CMC）	21	14.50%

（ *to be continued* ）

Topics for Discussion	Quantity	Ratio
Study on Students	21	14.50%
Development of Teaching Courseware	19	13.10%
Application of New Technologies	18	12.40%
Multimedia Applications	11	7.60%
Corpus Applications	10	6.90%
Online Learning	9	6.20%
Study on Teachers	7	4.80%
Others	4	2.80%
Total	145	100%

However, its broadness means that because computer technology is the core technology in the system of modern information technology （multimedia, computation, storage and communications technology, etc.）, the computer-based foreign language teaching technology can be reflected in almost every link of the foreign language course system, covering resources exploration, environment improvement, teaching design, teaching evaluation, product manufacture and so on. In fact, the elements of all sorts shown in the table are still not beyond these links.

Actually there is a group of scholars who have made continuous studies of CALL, especially the aspects of its educational theory, research horizons, objectives, methods, evaluation and research paradigm and so on. With their promotion, the study of CALL is on its way to a gradually mature research from the international viewpoint. The research fruits by stages are sufficient for examining the development status of world CALL. Scholars represented by Warschauer, M. & Healey, D.（1998）, Carol Chapelle（2000）, George M. Jacobs, Joy L. Egbert（2005）, Mike levy（1997, 1999, 2006, 2010）, Robert Debski（2003）, Robert J. Blake（2007）, Thomas S. C. Farrell（2001）, Philip Hubbard（2008）, Yong Zhao（1996）, etc. have either contributed articles or produced works with devoted efforts to explore more in-depth study of CALL, making a further step to the study of CALL.

Some scholars have touched upon the issues on cyber-based learning environment which focus on the cyber-based autonomous learning, learning strategies, etc. Different scholars have made various summaries of cyber-based learning environment.

Bandrul H. Khan （2002）, the chief editor of American journal *Educational Technology* believed that a meaningful learning environment constituted many factors which were interrelated and mutually independent. He was in the opinion that the construction of a network learning environment required eight aspects, namely system, education, technology, interface design, evaluation, management, resource support and ethics.

Tolboom （2003） considered that "network-based learning environment is the integrality of hardware, software and educational activities which during the process of Internet using are to support and organize learning processes and promote exchange activities".

While Wikipedia defines network-based learning environment as an environment system which is established for facilitating teachers' management on students during the teaching process, especially a kind of system includes computer hardware and software, distance learning also involved. In North America, the network-based learning environment is often regarded as "Learning Management System" （LMS for short）.

2.1.1.2 Domestic Research of CALL

If the time extension is set from 1979 to 2002, CNKI will tell you that there are 60 papers on the given theme of "computer-assisted language learning". If considering the delay of the time of article writing, publication, and uploading electronic draft, adding one more year from 1979 to 2003, the search results would read 77 papers. According to the search, the interdisciplinary subjects are 8 from foreign language words, computer software and computer application, education theory and education management, Chinese language and words to higher education, etc. The literature types only cover periodicals, meetings and master's thesis.

Under the same condition, if the time is set from 2004 to 2010 （a year later）, and the results showed that the articles totaled 209. It is quite clear that the number is increasing. The number in the latter six years is twice more than that in the previous 24 years. From the annual average contribution, the former period averaged 3.2 articles per year, while the latter period ballooned to 34.8 articles per year. The generation reports added one more type that is Ph.D. thesis to this literature type. The articles on "foreign language literature" totaled 81, whose ratio ranked a lot, among the eight interdisciplinary subjects with an increase of one tenth to nearly a third.

Domestic scholars have made researches on the exploration of informationized foreign language teaching and reflected on the modernization of foreign language teaching. With the rapid development of educational technologies since the new period onward and the absorption of the essence of its technology-based teaching theory, another batch of outstanding research works are produced in the field of foreign language teaching. The representative works are as follows:

Educational Technology and Foreign Language Teaching （Dai Zhengnan & Huang Guangyuan, 1998）, *Modern Educational Technology and Modern Foreign Language Teaching* （He Gaoda, 2002）, *The Application of Computers in English Education* （Chen

Hong & Liu Beili, 2005）, *Computers and English Teaching—from Theory to Practice*（Gu Yueguo, 2006）, *Computer-assisted Foreign Language Learning—Theory and Practice*（Jia Guodong, 2007）, *Computer-assisted Second Language Research Methodology and Its Application*（Wang Lifei, 2007）, *Information Technology and Foreign Language Teaching*（Liu Risheng, et al., 2007）, *Foreign Language Teaching Technology*（Cheng Dongyuan, 2008）, *The Theory of Modern Linguistics and Multimedia Foreign Language Teaching*（Zeng Fangben, 2010）, *The Integrated Course of Modern Education Technology and Foreign Language Teaching*（Wen Heping, et al., 2010）, *The Integration of Computers and Networks into Foreign Language Curriculum*（Chen Jianlin, 2010）, *The Research of Information Technology and Foreign Language Teaching—Theoretical Construction and Practical Exploration*（Chen Jianlin, Hu Jiasheng, 2010）, and other relevant works authorized by Mei Deming（1990, 2003）, Hu Zhuanglin（2006, 2007）, Wang Shouren（2008, 2009）, Dai Weidong & Hu Wenzhong（2009）, Gu Peiya（2006）, Wang Qi（2006）, Zhang Hongling（2010）, Zhang Bomin（2006）, etc.

2.1.2 Research Status of Cyber-based Foreign Language Ecological Teaching & Ecological Environment

2.1.2.1 Research Status Abroad

In 1932, the American educator W. Waller put forward "ecology of classroom" in the course of Teaching Sociology, which marked the official use of "ecology" in education study. In 1940s, Midwest Psychological Field Station held by R. Barker and H. Wright from University of Kansas was the ecological research center on human behavior. In 1967, the term "educational ecology" was first advanced in Public Education by Lawrence Cremin, the rector of Teachers College of Columbia University. In 1970s, U. Bronfenbrenner from Cornell University tried to establish a study of "ecology of human development". Most of these studies focused on the relations between individual behavior and environment in the school situation. During this period, particular concern fell on the ecology research of school environment. British scholar Eggleston J. showed great ingenuity in School Ecology（1977）by studying the distribution of education resources as the subject. In 1980s and 1990s, the idea that school was a "cultural ecosystem" was first proposed by J. Goodlad from the University of Washington in 1987, and the eco-educator C. A. Bowers made further research about educational ecology problems including school micro ecology（such as classroom teaching）, culture, ecological crisis and some other issues. At the beginning of this century, "The Dynamic Nature of Language Classroom" published by Tudor in 2001 together with "The Ecology of Language

Acquisition" published by Leather in 2003, marked the formal formation of ecological foreign language classroom teaching. Foreign scholars were quite inconsistent in the study object of educational ecology; however, they all emphasized the basic spirit of ecology: integration, connection and balance. The study mainly focused on three factors: micro-educational ecology, educational ecology of ecological factors, macro-educational ecology. Micro-educational ecology studied the ecological environment of school and the ecological environment of classroom as well as the impact on individual behavior and education; educational ecology of ecological factors studied main ecological factors that can bring influence on the development and change within the educational ecosystem; macro educational ecology treated education as a functionally coordinated ecosystem with boundary, range and level. To be specific, it focused on the constituent elements, features, functions, operation mechanism, etc. （Fan Gaorui, 1995:89）

2.1.2.2 Domestic Research

◆ 2.1.2.2.1 Related Works

Domestic concerns about educational ecology started relatively late. In 1960s, Fang Binglin from the Department of Education, Taiwan Normal University, began his research in this field and published the book *Ecological Environment and Education*. In the late 1980s, Li Congming from Taiwan, published the book *Introduction to Educational Ecology*. In the book, thinking over the reality of education in Taiwan, he employed principles of ecology and reflected on the various educational elements. In 1990, *Educational Ecology* was published by Wu Dingfu and Zhu Wenwei. It was the first book in this field in mainland China, involving basic principles of educational ecology, the basic law of educational ecology, education resources and educational ecology, behavioral ecology of education, ecological distribution of school, ecological environment of school, ecological environment of classroom and the sustainable development strategy of educational ecology and so on. In 1992, Ren Kai published *Educational Ecology*, hoping to make profound analysis of education phenomenon by using ecological principles and methods （He Zubin, 2005）. In 2000, Fan Guorui published *Educational Ecology*. On the discipline system of constructivism, the book strived to elaborate education ecology from culture, population, resources as well as environment. It cited a large number of foreign research results and compared these results with comparative approach. In 2010, Chen Jianlin published *The Integration of Computer Networks and Foreign Language Courses—A Study Based on College English Teaching Reform*. With detailed first-hand information, the book made an in-depth discussion on the hotspot of "Integration of Computer Networks and Foreign Language Courses" from the angles of course orientation, teaching mode, teachers' role, three-dimensional teaching material development as well as ecologicalization study of foreign language course. The book brought forward some constructive opinions.

◆ 2.1.2.2.2   Related Articles

In China's academic journals, a large number of research papers on English ecological education have been published. Qin Chen （2005） proposed that the application of ecological education in foreign language classroom was not simply the transplant of ecological terms, but a profound understanding of holism in ecological teaching. Tan Wei （2009） pointed out that the construction of an eco-class of college English should follow the principles as below: upholding student–centered concept, creating harmonious learning atmosphere, constructing a relaxed self-learning environment, and establishing interactional teacher-student relationship. Chen Xingli （2010） analyzed the possible problems existing in college English education reform and suggested that efforts and attempts could be made in concepts, management system, evaluation system, examination, test methods and accurate ecological niche to implement the reform. Sheng Renze （2008）, by referring to principles of ecological education, tried to reflect on college English multimedia class from the aspects of teaching environment, teaching modes, teaching monitoring, etc.

Many domestic researches have also been conducted on the application of ecology in foreign language class under multimedia network environment. The typical ones are: Chen Jianlin （2006） explored the characteristics of computer-assisted language learning and analyzed the position of computer in the new teaching mode from ecological perspectives, pointed out that if computer was only used as an assisting tool, it was impossible to achieve the reform goal. Only by an overall integration of computer networks into a foreign language curriculum could it be finally fulfilled; Liu Senlin （2008） advocated an ecological-based approach to the reform of college English curriculum design, classroom-based teaching strategies and ecological monitoring system. Their researches focused on constructing an integrated network of classroom ecosystems; Yang Zhou （2004） explored the differences of ecological teaching efficiency between multimedia classroom and traditional classroom, and made an analysis of the results aiming to illustrate the positive role of the multimedia teaching in the ecological teaching; Gao Fan, Zhang Yuanyuan （2010） held the view that the theory of ecological education should be put into all aspects of foreign language teaching. They advocated a new concept of education—using an ecological point of view to study college English phenomenon, as well as using principles of ecological education to construct an ecological classroom with the integration of network-based college English autonomous learning into classroom teaching from aspects of teaching environment, teaching mode and teaching monitoring, etc.; Dai Xiaohua （2009） pointed out that the course website, QQ group, mailing list, blog, etc. might be used to solve the current ecological teaching problems like limits of teaching resources and teaching time, etc. Besides, interactive teaching could stimulate learners' interest in learning and cognitive enthusiasm, broadening learners' scope of knowledge, and training learners' teamwork spirit and innovation ability; An Qi （2009） carried out an empirical research on conducting an ecological reform of college English teaching. Based on the analysis of all investigations, it was stated that the teaching reform of foreign language required the establishment of an ecological system; Hu Yuhui （2010）, whose ideas based on the principles of ecological education, proposed that the construction of an open classroom environment was conducive to network-based English class teaching and it was significant to promote interactive teaching, conducting student-centered classroom teaching targeting at students' sustainable development, and fully explored the system resources, hoping to give full play to the holism of ecological education system and as a result to improve English classroom teaching.

The papers on foreign language learners' ecological environment are published on many different journals. Some of them are listed and reviewed as follows:

On the study of learners' ecological environment :

In the paper "The Ecological Problems and Solutions in Virtual Learning Environment", Zhang Lixin & Zhang Lixia （2010） pointed out the present ecological problems in virtual learning environment, which according to the factors of virtual learning environment, could be summarized as three problems: short "life cycle" of physical environment, social environment with impersonal "interpersonal relationship" and immature regulatory environment. Some possible solutions to these three problems were suggested by them.

In the paper "The Analysis of Ecological Imbalance and Countermeasures in Virtual Learning Environment", Zhang Lixin & Li Hongmei （2009） studied the virtual learning environment from ecological perspective, in which many problems can be seen as the ecological imbalance. The imbalance of ecological virtual learning environment is featured in two aspects: the imbalance between ecological virtual learning environment and learners; the imbalance between internal structure and function. In their paper, two countermeasures in terms of internal self-regulatory mechanism and external preventive detection and protection system are recommended for the imbalance.

In the paper "Constructing Language Learning Environment on Learner-autonomy", Sun Hong （2004） stated that autonomous learning needed great supports of language environment. However, the reality on campus in China was not as ideal as expected. Besides, it focused on constructing learning environment and instructional design and proposed improvement measures accordingly in order to offer multiple English learning opportunities for students to use the language. Meanwhile, under the instruction of active learning and independent study, students were expected to choose the appropriate learning methods based on individual needs and made good use of the teaching resources that the university provided to enhance their ability in English listening, speaking, reading, writing and translation.

In the paper "The Exploration of College English Teaching Reform", Huang Ruoyu （2000） analyzed the causes of integrating multimedia into teaching reform, experimental reforms and actual implementation of multi-media teaching. According to feedbacks from the teachers and students, a conclusion was made: multimedia foreign language teaching was new to both teachers and students. In the article, both the advantages and limitations of multimedia foreign language teaching were pointed out. As the article indicates, the biggest advantage of multimedia foreign language teaching was that it was conducive to the establishment of a student-centered teaching model.

An Qi （2009）, in the article "An Empirical Study Based on College English Teaching with the Background of Networks", made systemic analysis on the questionnaire based on the background of College English Teaching Reform and held the view that the establishment of ecological foreign language curriculum system was very necessary to foreign language teaching reform. In the end, some enlightenments were made by An Qi.

Zhang Lixia & Wang Wenli （2010）, in the article "The Construction of Virtual Learning Environment from Ecosystem Perspective", pointed out that due to the lack of ecological cognition of a virtual learning environment, ecological problems such as a waste of virtual resources, lifeless interactions, disorders, etc. emerged. Then the article, from the ecological point of view, regarded the virtual learning environment as an ecosystem, and described the ecological virtual learning environment to be systematic, dynamic, open and self-organized. In the end, some detailed measures were put forward with an attempt to guide the virtual learning environment to be harmonious, healthy and ecological by suggesting some new concepts in the designing and development, operation and management of the learning environment.

The study of cyber-based ecological environment for foreign language learners can be seen as follows:

Li Lixin （2002: 28-30） stated that online learning environment consists of all the external conditions indispensable for the existence of network learning system including network learning resources, online learning community, and all other network learning system.

Wang Jing （2005） expounded that the connotation of network learning environment could be interpreted from both broad and narrow sense. In a broad sense, the network learning environment referred to the learning environment created by network-based study areas and learning media, while the network learning environment in a narrow sense mainly meant the platform of online communication supported by application software, programming language, aiming to provide students with learning materials.

Zhang Lixin & Li Hongmei （2009：17-20） expounded that the network-based learning environment, also known as eco-virtual learning environment, which could reflect the ecological laws and principles, were featured by self-control, self-improvement, and self-development. Being student-centered, it could impose direct or indirect impact on learners' learning with the integration of various factors.

As for the compositions or components of learning environment, different scholars have different views. Zhou Yanan（2005: 41-43）thought that: network-based learning environment consisted of three parts: Firstly, the material environment, which was the material basis for the existence of the network because a network-based learning system must be attached to a computer and related equipment. Secondly, information resource environment, which was the core environment of network-based learning ecological environment because resources were the underlying value of a network-based learning ecosystem. The strengths and weaknesses of network-based learning eco-environment could be reflected by information resource environment. A good learning environment always had an easy access to resources. Thirdly, the social environment. Here, social environment specifically referred to the social environment with sensitive factors, closely related to network-based learning development and composed of network laws and regulations, network learning ethics, social education, science and technology, economic development and so on.

Zhang Lixin & Li Shigai（2008: 5-8）pointed out that the physical environment, social environment and regulatory environment formed a virtual learning eco-environment. The physical environment included various learning materials from virtual space. It was comprised of "hardware resources, software resources and information resources" and was the final presentation in front of learners for all kinds of learning activities. Social environment was the relationship among learners during the virtual learning process. Social environment reflected three interpersonal relationships between learners and other learners, learners and facilitators, as well as learners and administrators. Regulatory environment referred to all sorts of rules and regulations made to ensure the smooth development of learners' activities by forming learning atmosphere, learning culture, learning attitudes, learning values during the virtual learning process, eventually shaping into a mechanism for learning and moral restraint.

Su Xiaohua（2006）proposed that the network-based learning environment was composed of physical environment, technological environment and regulatory environment. She especially marked out that technological environment included four sub-environments: information resource environment, interactive and cooperative environment, management and monitoring environment, and evaluation and incentive environment while regulatory environment was comprised of humanistic environment and emotional-psychological environment.

In "Ecological Management of Education", Wu Linfu（2006）stated the environment of ecological education was a complex environment with natural environment, social environment and regulatory environment.

On the explorations of students' autonomous learning ability, motivation, strategy and teaching mode within network teaching environment:

In the paper "Study on Leaner Autonomy of English Majors in Web-based Environment", Liu Jinxia (2009) first indicated that how to instruct and monitor the English majors' learner autonomy was an urgent issue for the teachers to solve in web-based environment. Then he discussed the problems from changing the teachers' attitude towards teaching, perfecting evaluating system to guiding students how to use learning strategies and ways of internal monitoring to learn autonomously.

In the paper "Motivation Orientation in a Web-Based Environment", Liu Wenyu & Zha Ji'an (2009) first made an analysis that the fundamental baseline of affecting learning outcomes lied in the motivation orientation of the students. The students' motivation orientation to learning included their intrinsic and extrinsic orientation, task value, control of learning beliefs, self-efficacy for learning and performance, and test anxiety. Then the study examined the relationship of English learners' motivation orientation towards learning in a web-based environment. Different dimensions on the motivation orientation of 180 students across three educational levels from Dalian University of Technology were assessed and compared by using MLSQ. The results showed that the students' responses across the three educational levels were rather homogenous.

In the paper "A Study on the Relationship Between Performance in CET-4 in an Internet and Multimedia Environment and Language Learning Strategies", Sun Qiudan & Huang Fang (2010) attempted to illustrate the relationship between language learning strategies (LLS) and performance in College English Test (CET) Band 4 of Chinese non-English major undergraduate students studying in the Internet and multimedia environment. A survey based on Oxford's (1990) Strategy Inventory for Language Learning (SILL) was administered to 238 first-year non-English majors from Peking University Health Science Center. The Statistical Package for Social Sciences (SPSS) 13.0 was used to analyze the data. The findings of the research suggested that the total CET-4 scores of the students were significantly related with direct learning strategies, including cognitive strategies, memory strategies and compensation strategies. The study also showed that in the Internet and multimedia environment, the listening scores of higher achievers were closely related to the five categories of strategies, namely, cognitive strategies, compensation strategies, affective strategies, memory strategies and social strategies, while the relationship of lower achievers' listening scores and their learning strategies did not show a correlation pattern. Suggestions were discussed for further improvement of Internet and computer-based language instruction, especially when it came to strategy training for the students.

In the paper "On the Characteristics of Multimedia Computer Assisted Language Learning", Yang Chunhui (2000) summarized and discussed the five characteristics of multimedia computer-assisted language learning (MCALL), concluding that the new teaching mode of student-centered in MCALL allowed students to conduct exploratory learning in individualized learning environment, thus improving learning efficiency. It was also pointed out that the findings will remind teachers of the five beneficial characteristics of MCALL during their teaching process, and help to avoid some shortcomings of traditional English teaching, thus making full and effective use of multimedia computer-assisted language learning.

In the paper "Constructivism and Multimedia-assisted College English Teaching", Zhang Xiaoying & Li Tianxian (2002) explored three multimedia-assisted college English teaching patterns on the basis of constructivism: classroom teaching pattern, individual pattern and network pattern. The changes and existing problems caused by these patterns were also discussed.

The environment that foreign language learning ecosystem identified is a comprehensive, dynamic and balanced environment. It has a compatible relationship between various elements within the system, which comes from the characteristics of ecological environment; it can restrain students' learning activities so that all factors can interact and interchange with each other, which comes from the characteristics of systemic theory; it can influence individuals' personal development, which comes from the environmental outlook of environmental psychology; it can promote cultural development, which comes from the cultural characteristics of educational environment. Therefore, an ideal foreign language learning environment should focus on two basic principles: first, to maintain stable learning structure with compatible learning elements; second, to restrict functioning of students' learning and promote individuals' development.

◆2.1.2.2.3　Related Projects

Taiwan has first witnessed the establishment of an institution specialized in ecological education. The purpose of its establishment is to have a general idea about the characteristics of people and factors in ecological education environment and explore their mutual relationships, thus understanding better the development of education. At the same time, it also aims to conduct researches on ecological education environment from a comprehensive, systematic, transcendental, integrated perspective, thus achieving its in-depth analysis. The research objects include students and parents by studying their physiology and psychology, as well as the relationship between society, culture and education.

In addition, some mainland schools carried out related research projects on ecological education. For example, in 2008, Li Jinbo chaired the significant project granted by the Planning Office of "Eleventh Five-Year Plan", National Education Science. The project was one of

Ministry of Education's key projects named "Comprehensive Assessment and Prediction of Cognitive Load Through Digital Learning" (Grant No.: DCA080141).

In 2005, Professor Fan Guorui chaired one of the major projects granted by Key Research Base of Humanities & Social Sciences, Ministry of Education. The subject was "Ecological Research on School Education: System Construction & Cultural Generation" (Grant No.: 05JJD880060).

In 2007, Wang Quanlin's project "An Ecological Study on College Teachers' Scholarism: Constructive Perspective of Critical Culture" (Grant No.: DIA070114) was approved by the Planning Office of "Eleventh Five-Year Plan", National Education Science.

In 2004, Professor He Gaoda from South China Agricultural University chaired the one of the first expansion projects of College English Teaching Reform granted by Ministry of Education. The subject was "A Study on Adaptability of College English Teaching in Multimedia Environment" (Grant No.: [2004] 250, Department of Higher Education, Ministry of Education).

In mainland China, the study of education ecology takes on four orientations. One focuses on the relationship between education and ecological environment; the second tendency is towards the study of education ecological system; the third orientation is mainly about research projects; the fourth tendency is towards its practical application. The four tendencies have laid a good foundation for the further study of education ecology and they are valuable explorations for the establishment of education ecology. However, the construction and optimization of ecological environment for foreign language learners is still in the blank under the background of computer networks.

◆ 2.2 ◆
Theoretical Framework

Due to constructing foreign language learners' ecological environment within the multi-media network environment related to Computer-assisted Language Learning, this study will analyze the connection and seek the support from the theories of Cognitivism, Constructivism, Ecology Theory, the relevance theory of multimedia information technology and foreign language teaching.

2.2.1 CALL

CALL is the shortened form of Computer-assisted Language Learning. Computers coordinated to people's arranged language teaching plan and content can facilitate in-class teaching and after-class practice. CALL can be divided into four types: （1） tuitional type, （2） the training type, （3） simulated type, （4） the tool type. The running courseware can form the environment of CALL which has the following four advantages in education: （1） Autonomously setting the pace. Students' learning ability will naturally determine the speed of courseware process, truly realize "teaching students in accordance with their aptitude". （2） Reducing the students' psychological burden. Computer doesn't show any emotion, so its patient induction and careful encouragement for students can help them to achieve the desired effect. （3） The courseware can take in teachers' and experts' strong points. （4） Facilitating the accumulation of teaching materials and the preservation of students' files.

2.2.2 The Relevance Between Information Technology and Foreign Language Teaching and Learning

The main content of information technology is firstly featured by its sensing technology （such as sensor, identification and transmission technology）. The information carrier takes a variety of forms, such as movies, television, image, records, voice, books, newspapers, periodicals, graphics, etc. To sum up, it can be divided into three major functional modules: image （static or dynamic）, text and sound, which are the three forms of "genealogy". Therefore, the form of information technology will include all contents of language or language teaching, conforming to the form of foreign language teaching as well as to the feature of informationization of foreign language, creating prerequisites for connecting marriage between foreign language teaching activities and information technology.

Computers have witnessed its high-quality information technologies like audio-visual procession technique, with which the basic language teaching skills are obviously reflected. This has provided the best conditions for language teaching and learning ability, enabling the correspondence of sensory function and psychological cognition between the five skills of listening, speaking, reading, writing, translating and the occurrence and development of technology. The combination and close blending between foreign language classroom teaching and information technology have shown the natural and essential relevance between the two parts.

In recent decades, with the development of multimedia network technology, the multimedia foreign language teaching—including all kinds of cyber-based teaching methods—will be inevitably presented by means of multimedia, gradually becoming a mainstream of teaching technology. And the most striking feature of multimedia foreign language teaching is still based on visual and auditory cognitions, so under the multimedia background, the foreign language learning still reflects the features of "Generative Theory of Multimedia Learning" by Meyer, accordance with his conclusive "ten laws of multimedia learning" (Yan Zhiming, 2008).

According to the above illustrations of the relationship between information technology and foreign language teaching and learning, it is clearly seen that the following characteristics are reflected during the process of fusion between information technology and foreign language learning.

Ontology. It is kind of ontological transfer and exchange of language information, the means of language information being its carrier, that is to say, it is kind of information communication within language itself by means of language.

Closure. All the teaching content and teaching process can be done just by means of information. In other words, only depending on the information technology can complete the teaching task smoothly, with no need of extra materialized auxiliary. This is decided by the uniqueness of information technology because all the information of language teaching can be shown, transmitted and communicated through information technology. As a matter of fact, the means of information was first produced for the purpose of exchanging language information.

Informationization. Language is the carrier of information, as well as one part of the information. The exchange and conversion of information is actually the exchange and conversion of language materials. Language teaching is kind of information exchange of language materials as well as kind of generative practices. Therefore, during this process, the language is informationized, such as the informational, artistic and technical procession of words and sound, after which comes the interactive communication.

Integration. The means of information technology are functionally compatible with the requirements of language information communication and exchange, which can fully help complete the task of language teaching and learning. As for this informationized and technologized teaching behavior, the information technology and the information itself are ontologically interdependent through beneficial interaction, forming a complete entirety which can be seen in the procession of language pronunciation and illustrations, organically integrated.

Due to the complicated and varied role of computer information technology in the learning of foreign language, computer information technology can not only be regarded as the tools and environment but also the means and elements, hence it exerts a subtle influence. Apart from that, it has a catalytic effect of "technological enzyme", which can penetrate into every link of foreign language teaching.

The biggest role of information technology in foreign language teaching and learning is to optimize the foreign language teaching, including its teaching design, teaching management, development, assessment, the development of teaching materials, the training of teachers' teaching skills and the enhancement of students' learning skills and proficiency.

As for the simple forms of learning links and learning content, it may be reflected in concrete and tangible technology means, such as the study of audio-visual course; while in comparatively complex learning process and subjects, it might not be easily sensed by students about the information technology, such as data-driven vocabulary learning, the compilation of teaching materials, and the layout as well as the design of courses, etc.

The use of technology will be manifested in organic integration between itself and various teaching and learning links, such as the arrangement, identification, organizational design and editing process of teaching resources; the artistic design, the presentation of teaching procedures, the interaction of main learning subjects, the evaluation of learning effect of in-class learning; the study of learning content—language itself, and so on. All contents are deeply implanted by technological genes, making foreign language learning rely heavily on information technology, almost in every step.

2.2.3 Cognitivism (Learning Theory)

Cognitivism (Learning Theory) comes from the theory originated by Gestalt School, which held the view that learning is a process of forming and developing cognitive structures through positive organization in learners' mind under the current situation. The theory of cognitivism also emphasizes that the relation among stimulation reactions is based on the medium of consciousness, focusing on the importance of cognitive process.

The representatives of cognitive structure theory are Swiss psychologist named J. Piaget and American psychologist named J.S. Bruner. Both of them maintained that cognition structure referred to the knowledge structure in learners' mind, which covered learners' complete views or the contents and organizations of views within the scope of learners' knowledge.

They considered that learning could lead to the combination between new materials or new experience and old materials or past experience, thus forming an internal knowledge structure, namely the cognitive structure. Piaget also pointed out that the structure was reflected in the forms of figure, assimilation, adaptation and balance, while Bruner held the view that learning didn't lie in the passive formation and response but in the active forming of cognitive structure. Learning consisted of a series of processes, so much attention should be paid to the study of students' learning behavior and the basic structure of each subject in the process of teaching. They attached great importance to the teaching materials of knowledge structure. The school also systematically elaborated the cognitive structure and its relationship with the classroom teaching. The recent years' teaching practices and experimental researches showed that the intentional means of controlling learners' cognitive structure can not only improve the availability, stability, clarity and distinction of cognitive structures but also play an effective role in solving certain kinds of learning problems.

Cognitivism （learning theory） has provided theoretical basis for teaching theories. It has enriched the study of education psychology and has greatly promoted the development of education psychology. The main contributions are as follows:

2.2.3.1　Paying attention to the subjective value of people in various learning activities and fully affirm the learners' conscious dynamic role.

2.2.3.2　Emphasizing the important position and role of conscious activities, such as cognition, connotation understanding, independent thinking, etc. in learning activities.

2.2.3.3　Paying attention to people's preparation in learning activities, that is, a personal learning effect not only depends on external stimulation and individual subjective effort, but also depends on one's existing knowledge level, the cognitive structure and the non-cognitive factors. Preparation is the premise for any meaningful learning activity.

2.2.3.4　Focusing on the role of reinforcement. Cognitivism seriously emphasize the role of reinforcement brought by its intrinsic motivation and learning activities because of its consideration of students' learning as a kind of positive process.

2.2.3.5　Advocating the creation of learning creativities. Bruner's learning theory of discovery emphasized the students' learning flexibility, initiative and discovery. It required that learners should observe, explore and carry out experiments, carry forward the spirit of creation, think independently, reorganize materials, and try to discover the principles of knowledge. So it advocated an inquiring and zetetic learning method which meant that learning discoveries made learners cultivate their potential wisdom, adjust and strengthen their learning motivation, and helped them firmly master knowledge and the innovation ability.

2.2.4　Constructivism（Learning Theory）

Contemporary constructivists argue that the world is in its objective existence, but the understanding and meaning of the world is decided by each person. We construct reality with our own experiences, or rather we interpret the reality. Everyone's experience is created by his own brain. Because of our different beliefs and experience, we understand the world differently. Therefore, learning does not mean the simple passing of teachers' knowledge on to learners, but means the learners' own construction of knowledge. Learners are not passively receiving information, but actively constructing knowledge. The construction is irreplaceable by others.

The learning process includes two aspects of construction: one is the construction of meaning towards new information, which also covers the reform and reorganization of its original experience. This is consistent with Piaget's two-way construction process through assimilation and realization.

It is just that constructivists attach more importance to the latter construction, which emphasizes that the learners do not rely on the pattern of activity or the proposition network extracted in their learning process. Instead, their understanding of concepts is rich and experience-based which can be used to flexibly construct the pattern of new learning activity.

Learning certainly involves learners' original cognition structure and learners will understand and construct new knowledge and information based on his own past experience, including irregular study before formal study and ordinary concepts before the study of scientific concepts. Learning is not passively receiving information, but actively constructing its meaning and forming new meaning by active selection, procession and disposal of external information, according to their experience background. External information itself has no meaning, and the meaning is constructed through its repeated and two-way interaction between the old and new knowledge and experience. Therefore, the study is not like the behaviorism description of the "stimulate-reaction" formula. The acquisition of meaning is based on learners' original knowledge or experience, then on the recognition and coding of new information, and finally on the construction of their own understanding. In this process, learners' original knowledge will be adjusted and changed due to the injection of new knowledge and experience. So, what constructivists cared about is the knowledge construction based on the original experience, psychological structure and faith.

2.2.5 Ecology Theory

2.2.5.1 Ecology and Fundamentals of Ecology

Ecology is the science of studying the relationships of interconnection and interaction of various factors between living organisms and their environments. Based on etymological trace, the word "ecology" originated from German word *Ökologie* which was formed by Greek *etyma Öikos* (meaning "home" or "residential place") and German *etyma logie* (meaning "study"). Home is a complex compound of relations. Regarding ecology as "home" totally embodies the relationships structure: integral, entirety, and system. The structure not only has close relation to living, life and production, but also with features of totality, integrity and versatility.

Research ranging from Ecology to the Natural Science of Ecology is a big step forward in the history of human beings. This discipline experienced the establishment and development period from the early 17th century to 1950s, during which it transformed itself gradually from ecological observation on individual species to group studies, and moved onto the ecological system studies. A large group of ecologists presented various valuable theories and devoted themselves into diversifying the discipline with different sub-disciplines. For example, Boyle's （1670） studied on the influence of lower pressure on animals marked the beginning of Zooecology; Reaumur（1735） established Insect Ecology by contributing to the research of physiological relations between temperature and insect growth; Humboldt（1807）, the founder of Geobotany and Phytocoenology, made remarkable researches on the distribution of vegetation, as well as appearances and characteristics of communities based on climates and geographic factors; Darwin（1859） and his world-known masterpiece *Origin of Species* tremulously pushed forward the development of Ecology and the *Theory of Evolution*; Haeckel （1866） was the first one who ever defined Ecology as the science of studying the interrelation between organisms and their environments. Ecology was defined in this way for over a hundred years and laid a solid groundwork for ecological scientific study. Following it, other definitions have been proposed, like Möbius'（1877） biocoence concept, Schröter's（1910） autecology and group ecology, Johnson's ecological niche term and Grinell's （1917） definition to the term afterwards, Ekton's（1927） Food Chain theory, Tansley's（1935） definition of Ecosystem, Thienemann's（1939） relation theories among producers, consumers, and decomposers, Birge et al.'s（1941） Energy Revenue and Expenditure concept and Lindemann's （1942）Energy Flow Theory about ecosystem and so on.

Generally speaking, the fundamentals of Ecology are rich, including study range of Ecology, principles of ecosystem, theory of restriction factors, theories on the structure and level of individual, group and community, development and evolution of ecosystem, and so on. Because fundamentals have a developing and improving process, fundamentals of Ecology is no exception. Although Bioecology, Human Ecology, Social Ecology, Ecology of Education have different studying targets and principles, they share the same mother discipline—Ecology, which determines the same fundamentals are applied in all of them. Therefore, considering the research shall be with an emphasized area, only the common fundamentals that both natural ecosystem and social ecosystem abide by are discussed in this paper.

Expansion and adaption principle: the development of any enterprise, region or sector has its own specific resources ecological niche. Successful development demands good expansion of resources ecological niche, so as to transform and adapt to the environment. Expansion without adaption lacks stability and flexibility of development, while adaption without expansion lacks speed and force.

Growth and restraint principle: any system has some favorable factors or some restraint factors, leading its development or limiting its development; the scarcity of resources leads to competition and intergrowth mechanism within the system. This role of intergrowth is to improve the utilization efficiency of resources, enhances the system's autogenic vitality and makes sustainable development. A system lack of any mechanism is not a vital system.

Ecological development principle: development is a process of progressive and orderly systematic development and function perfecting. The target of systematic succession lies in the perfection of function, not the growth of structure or elements; the systematic production aims at the service efficiency to the society, rather than the quantity or quality of the product.

Coincidence principle: systematic development's risk and opportunity are balanced. Great opportunities are often accompanied by high risk. Good ecosystem should be good at seizing every appropriate opportunity to use all available and even confrontational, harmful power to serve the system by turning the harm into a benefit.

Cumulative impact principle: a past or current project or act will impact on the ecosystem, even if this project or act is individual or negligible. After a certain period, they will also produce significant, enormous response, that is, cumulative effect.

In short, from some point of view, these principles have interpreted the law of change and development of things in different circumstances, in which, fundamentally speaking, there are two ecological concepts penetrating—the concept of ecosystem and the concept of dynamic balance.

2.2.5.2 Ecosystem

Ecosystem is also translated as "ecological system", the particular space combination of life system and environmental system. Within an ecosystem, there is a balance between various living things and environments. If any alien species or substance invades this ecosystem, the balance will be destroyed, and consequently another balance may gradually be reached. However, if the balance of the ecosystem is seriously damaged, the imbalance may be permanent. Balance of the ecosystem is a dynamic balance, reflecting the law of variation of the internal total quantities, and the individual should comply with the motion balance rules. Dynamic balance of things is relative rather than absolute, motorial rather than static, changing rather than eternal. It is a matter of internal self-regulation. It is the result generated by the comprehensive movement of all the individuals inside the living things.

Along with the development of ecosystem, relevant concepts have been brought up to the discipline, revealing the laws and mechanism of ecosystem, including ecological balance, dissipative structure, ecological niche and the integrity of ecosystem. Ecosystem, ecological balance and ecological niche are all important concepts now. Ecosystem refers to the basic natural and open ecological unit that is formed by organism and environment in a certain space. In this unit, all living organism compete with, act against and rely on each other, which gradually forms a healthy and ordered state of environment. The fundamental features of an ecosystem are diversified structures, complicated system, flowing energy, circulating material and dynamic and self-adjustable system. Ecological balance is an inferior concept of ecosystem, referring to an ecosystem that under some specific conditions and through passing and exchange between internal and external parts in terms of material, energy and information, can reach a coordinated and unified state in which interrelations between living things inside the system and the relations between living things and the environment exist in mutual understanding and harmony. The above-mentioned state is self-controllable, self-adjustable and develops itself in a natural way. In other words, ecological balance is the top-level stable state of an ecosystem from formation to maintenance. It is a relative and dynamic balance, based on relations and interactions between different parts inside the system, as well as between the system and the outside environment, which can be achieved through structures and functions that have been adjusting along development of ecosystem. Ecological niche is also known as the mini Ecology, which is the residence and career of any organism. Odum（1952）held the opinion that every organism owned itself a best existing position in space-time in the longstanding competitions—an ecological niche. The space-time position and state of any organism in group and ecosystem decide its pattern, physiological responses and special behaviors. There are some important inferior concepts below niche, including overlapping and competition, separation of niche, breadth of niche, compression and release of niche, removal of niche, dynamism of niche and so on. The concept and content of ecological niche's space-time, functions and multi-dimensional level resemble the activities of human being in society. Since 1990s, the theory of niche has become one of the most important basic ecological theories in the field, infiltrating more and more research areas and being applied increasingly wide. It is an advanced frontier subject in today's academia and overspreads continually.

2.3

Research Design

Literature review. The current study will make full use of research literatures at home and abroad on foreign language learners' ecological environment under the background of multimedia network. By relying on CALL theory, Cognitivism, Constructivism, Ecology and the Relevance Between Multimedia Information Technology and Foreign Language Learning, it aims to offer theoretical basis for constructing and optimizing foreign language learners' ecological environment under the background of multimedia networks. Moreover, possible research evidences are intended to be dug out through relevant literatures, firstly in order to make full use of existing research fruits and provide basic support and research foundation, and secondly to summarize and design a model of optimizing cyber-based ecological environment for foreign language learners through the relevant empirical research, constituting the conclusive part of the study.

Questionnaire. By using designed relevant questions, the author made surveys of college students' viewpoints on the four sub-ecological environments（namely physical learning environment, resourceful learning environment, technological learning environment and emotional learning environment）, their actual use of computers and networks in college English class, their perspective of teachers' role, students' role, and the positioning of computers, and the present situation of college students' autonomous English learning under the environment of networks and computers. With all of these, college students' actual needs are handy and their opinions or suggestions are collected. This kind of analysis is to provide relevant empirical basis for constructing and optimizing the model of cyber-based foreign language learners' ecological environment.

Comparative analysis. The conclusion drawn from this topic-based relevant empirical research will be compared with the existing research for verification of the existing related theories. By comparison, the new viewpoint will be shown, that is, a functionally balanced mode with all elements in appropriate ecological niches and the four sub-systems in harmony within the foreign language education system.

3
Chapter

Overview on Problems in Cyber-based Foreign Language Learners' Environment

According to the new "College English Curriculum Requirements" issued by Chinese Ministry of Education in 2007, it is stipulated that colleges and universities should make full use of modern information technology. It is also advocated that a cyber-and-classroom-based teaching mode should be adopted, in order to improve the traditional teacher-centered mode. The new teaching mode should rely on modern information technology, especially on network technology, enabling foreign language teaching and learning to be individualized and autonomic learning, as well as free from time and place restrictions.

The integration of computer networks into foreign language curriculum has changed the ways in information transference and acceptance, teaching content, and the organization of teaching activities during the process of traditional teaching. This has directly led to the alternation of teaching concept and changes in teaching values and evaluation criteria. All these changes are bound to break the balance of traditional teaching environment. Unexpected disorders and imbalances emerge, which are characterized by the following five aspects: inconformity between national education policies and the actual implementations in local schools; inconsistency between concept and practice; imbalance between technology and its application; maladjustment between new teaching mode and traditional teaching system; disturbance between teaching process and teaching management. What's more, the imbalance of teaching environment causes many disorders in students' learning environment. The application of information technology in foreign language education has a big effect on the construction of foreign language learners' cyber-based learning environment and also on foreign language learners' development. However, the current cyber-based learning environment is full of disorders and imbalances. In this paper, the author divides foreign language learners' cyber-based learning environment into four sub-environments: physical learning environment, resourceful learning environment, technological learning environment and emotional learning environment. The details of imbalances in these four environments are as follows:

3.1

Imbalances of Physical Learning Environment

Foreign language learners' physical learning environment includes natural environment and social environment. Some schools are located in downtown areas, with very poor surroundings and campus conditions. Moreover, there is always a big noise, little fresh air and insufficient sunshine in classroom, dorms, libraries and labs. Although Ministry of Education encouraged colleges and universities to establish self-learning centers under cyber-based environment, yet quite a lot of places cannot afford the computers or technological equipments due to the lack of funds, hence no available networks. For some colleges and universities, though there is good support for the purchase of computer and networks, problems of coordination do exist between school administration and teaching staff because teachers do not have the final say on computer rooms, resulting in the imbalance between teaching process and teaching management. Although some students can have access to network, too many disturbances confound students' effective learning. In current physical learning environment, imbalances also exist between national education policy and local institutions' implementations of the policy.

3.2

Imbalances of Resourceful Learning Environment

Resourceful learning environment includes those learning factors, such as learning mode, teaching materials, lesson plans, reference materials, books, web resources, etc. Imbalances of resourceful learning environment mean that most schools use three-dimensional text materials while the teachers are still using the traditional teacher-centered pedagogy in that the teaching concepts, methods, tools, and teaching assessment are all very traditional. What's worse, there are quite a number of teachers who hold the view that regular foreign language teaching can be without the use of computers and networks and that it is a waste of time on computer-based teaching preparation and a great burden on computer-based teaching. In a word, the current situation is in great contrast with what Ms. Wu Qidi（former vice minister of the Ministry of Education）proposed at the video conference on trial implementation of college English teaching reform in 2004. She mentioned that "the reform of current teaching mode is to change the traditional model characterized by teacher-textbook-chalk, student-blackboard as well as teacher-teaching, student-listening into an active and personalized learning mode featured by the integrated combination of computer（or networks）, teaching software and class."

On the other hand, teachers have some conception of advanced theories（such as constructivism, student-centered theory）, but they fail to activate these good theories. Moreover, their knowledge of computers is not compatible with the social development in ways that they are lack of confidence in technology-based teaching and there is still a long way to go before all teachers are trained to fulfill the requirements posed by foreign language teaching reform. The imbalances of teaching leads to the imbalance of foreign language learners' cyber-based ecological environment which covers the following aspects: students' learning is not autonomous and independent but still rely on the teacher-centered mode; learning materials are not designed according to individual development; network resources are with low utilization, resulting in considerable resource waste; learners do not receive regular trainings, thus they are unable to make full use of network resources.

◆ 3.3 ◆
Imbalances of Technological Learning Environment

Technological learning environment means that during the learning process, learners can freely choose learning theories and have a good supporting system with suitable interface design, thus stimulate learners' interest in learning and ensure each functional module to be well guided by the system. Technological learning environment can not only facilitate learners' leaps if they feel it necessary during the learning process, but also provide good opportunities for students' group discussion and collaborative learning. But currently, in many colleges and universities, the design of functional modules are not made according to students' differences, i.e., the modules do not fully reflect the individuality and take students' different levels into account. The modules do not improve low-level learners' foreign language competence and create opportunities for high-level learners' further development. This can be seen as the imbalance of technological learning environment. The ideal and balanced technological learning environment is one which can not only consolidate students' language foundations, but also help cultivate and develop their practical abilities, especially listening and speaking abilities. The balanced technological learning environment is one which can not only guarantee the stable improvement of students' foreign language proficiency, but also be of great help in students' independent and individualized learning, compatible with the needs of their individual professional development.

Meanwhile, in most colleges and universities, the abuse of multimedia has been a big issue under the computer-network-based environment. Regardless of the actual teaching needs, a variety of media are used blindly, resulting in the flooding of class information and the excess of invalid class information, which will both disperse students' attention and affect the achievement of teaching goals. Even in some schools, the situation that "where there is multimedia, there is a class" is still quite common. However, the so-called "multimedia courseware" is only simple words plus some pictures, which can be easily shown by a projector. It is undoubtedly a misuse of good technology for minor purposes and a waste of resources. The due value of computers and networks is unfulfilled. Multimedia has become veritably "superfluous".

In addition, the overloaded information has resulted in "disorientation" phenomenon which refers to the proposition that if human brain receives excessive information in a short time, then the human brain comes to a standstill. It is one of the advantages of computers to store large amounts of information. But some of our teachers overuse the computer technology when producing the courseware. For example, they exhaustively list all the detailed and trivial contents but have to speed up the information transmission due to the limited class periods. The only result is that students are forced to be surrounded by dazzling multimedia information, unable to encode and decode the due knowledge, which directly affects the students' understanding and mastery of its due content and meaning. This is "disorientation" under the cyber-based learning environment.

3.4
Imbalances of Emotional Learning Environment

The emotional learning environment consists of three parts: psychological factors, interpersonal interaction, and social recognition of learners. Psychological factors include learners' cognition, affective learning, learning attitude, learning methods, learning concepts, self-control in learning, etc.; the success of interpersonal interaction （including self-interaction） plays a considerable role in learners' self-learning; the adoption of learning strategies and learning methods have a direct impact on learners' learning efficiency and on social recognitions of learners.

036 | 外语学习者计算机网络生态环境优化研究 | On Optimizing the Cyber-based Ecological Environment for Foreign Language Learners

Psychological factors: members in learning community are separated in time and space, leading to greater distances among learners' emotional exchanges. The current cyber-based teaching concept is lack of learners' psychological feelings which directly affects learners' effective learning. In classes with the integration of computer networks into foreign language curriculum, there is no teachers' enthusiastic lecture and face-to-face explanation. In other words, for teachers, it is very difficult to give full play to their body movements and polished charm. For students, it is quite insufficient to feel teachers' affections and get effective guidance from their facilitators. For the class itself, the lack of interactive atmosphere prevents students from active participation in classroom discussion and learning. Besides, the integration causes students' inappropriate learning concepts and methods, as well as the lack of self-control ability in the new environment. The integration also makes students unable to be involved in effective and passionate learning and unable to keep sustainable attention, all because learners' learning concepts, motivation, emotion, and other psychological factors impose great influence on learning interest and initiative, as well as on good maintenance of learning time and learning efficiency. In the computer-network-based environment, the imbalance of psychological factors directly affects learners' cognitive development.

Interpersonal interactions: the computer-network-based foreign language learning involves continual interactions between learners and learning environment. But since the integration of computer networks into foreign language curriculum, the three kinds of interactions （between learners and learners, between learners and computers, and within learners themselves） are not fully achieved. That is to say, the comparing and sharing of information are not basically realized, which is a failure in learner-learner interaction; learners can not deal well with a variety of network tools and technologies to access learning materials and to acquire knowledge, which is a failure in learner-computer interaction; learners do not have a deep and thorough understanding of the content and cannot make the acquired new knowledge integrated with the existing cognitive structures, which is a failure in self-interaction.

Social recognition: "College English Curriculum Requirements" clearly stipulates that the design of college English curriculum should take advanced information technology into account, in order to promote the computer-network-based foreign language teaching, and to provide students with good language learning environment and conditions. However, the actual situation is not what to be expected. On the contrary, imbalances known as the so-called "disconnection" between "central requirement" and "local implementation" emerge. In other words, many colleges and universities do not fully implement the new items of requirements for the curriculum. For example, there are still many problems in the construction and operation maintenance of computers network in cyber-based learning environment, leading to the lack of good interactions among learners, the lack of a vigorous and dynamic learning environment, and the poor positioning of computer-network-based foreign language learning. In a word, there is low learning efficiency for learners in computer-network-based foreign language learning environment, which has inevitably and seriously hampered social recognitions of cyber-based foreign language learning. Or it is safe to say that, the fundamental reason for "poor social recognition or acceptance" is that the output of computers and networks (the quality of foreign language learning) is inconsistent with the investment in constructions of computers and networks.

As is discussed above, the four learning environments—physical learning environment, resourceful learning environment, technological learning environment and emotional learning environment, also called the sub-environments of computer-network-based foreign language learning environments—are seriously imbalanced which can be concluded as follows: the learning modes, concepts, learning methods, learning content, learning media, etc. are incompatible with the existing cyber-based learning conditions, teaching faculty, enrollment of students, management quality, and matching materials; learners' social environment, regulatory mechanisms, management, emotional and psychological factors, etc. are all more or less imbalanced. These imbalances or disorders undoubtedly have brought about an imbalanced information-technology-based learning environment, which is impossible to survive in the school's education system. These serious imbalances further indicate that it is extremely urgent to find out a new approach to re-examine the underlying causes and taking effective measures. Therefore, it is unlikely to do so by relying solely on traditional foreign language teaching and learning theories because the occurrence of imbalances has been a great challenge to these traditional theories.

4 Chapter

◆ 4.1 ◆
Basic Requirements for Its Optimization

Firstly, optimizing foreign language learners' cyber-based ecological environment requires a physical learning environment with multi-directional cooperation system and stable interaction. Environmental psychology tells us that all organisms have certain interactions with their environment, which is essential for the existence of vital life creatures. Therefore, we need to take the campus and its surroundings into considerations when optimizing the learning environment. As to schools' education groups, the spiritual construction of a school is of educational significance. The school buildings should be diversified and unified, peaceful and balanced. Seats of multimedia classrooms should be well arranged according to the individuals' diversified characteristics and their different studying needs. Diversity makes students active, uniformity makes them stable, and peace makes them comfortable while balance makes them honest. Schools should provide the students with a quiet learning environment and a convenient network environment. An environment with moderate colors is more conducive to students' thinking than that with warm colors. So the rooms for intellectual activities such as classrooms and libraries are particularly better to be designed with a moderate style. Classroom lighting, ventilation, acoustics, height of desks and chairs, all have a direct impact on students' physical and mental health, and learning outcomes. So the equipments should be checked and replaced on time. The buildings should be helpful to the development of students' sociability, in order to lead them to know the importance of learning with group activities. In addition, ecological factors of a school like books, teaching aids, instruments, showroom, biological corners, audio-visual network systems, are all related to students' all-round development. Equipments and arrangements can stimulate students' motivation to learn. As for school norms, school style, classroom atmosphere and learning style which can be seen as spiritual powers, they play an important role in the creation of an environment with cooperative and collaborative learning. From the ecological point of view, the school is a small environment in society, which is subject to a variety of ecological factors (including non-biological, biological, and human factors; physical and spiritual factors). Therefore, when optimizing imbalanced factors in school, we not only need fully consider the physical factors, but also consider those elements of school management, that is focusing on how to strengthen the management of media equipment, technical personnel, etc. It is intended to create a healthy and harmonious physical learning environment for students.

Secondly, optimizing foreign language learners' cyber-based ecological environment requires a resourceful learning environment with balanced input and output. Insufficient supply of learning resources for learners will affect the survival and development of ecological learning environment. Learning resources should have the features of diversity, sharing, effectiveness and reproducibility. Because the education system is an open system, in which continuous flow exists between materials and energy, and these elements interact with its eco-environment. An ecosystem establishes its steadiness or balance in a relatively stable "input-output" relationship. When all kinds of circulations within the learning eco-environment for foreign language learners have some setbacks and disorders, two ways can be taken into consideration in order to re-establish the balance. On the one hand, we need to introduce information and resources. On the other hand, we may rely on internal reform of the environment and organization transformation, based on which the ecological learning environment can carry out its self-regulation and regain its new balance. The input of learning resources into foreign language learners' ecological learning environment not only includes human inputs, such as teachers', students', teaching administrators', technicians', but also possess material inputs, such as those of network, books, teaching materials, and other teaching or leaning references. In addition, a variety of values and norms, such as technical trainings for teachers and students, regulations, normative system, are also important inputs. The output of cyber-based ecological learning environment from foreign language learners mainly refers to acquisitions, attitude alternations, technical preparations, behavioral changes, critical thoughts, emotional changes, etc. The learning process is a process of the energy conversion between the four learning sub-environments. Therefore, we can focus on foreign language learners, and research on the complex relationships between ecosystems as well as its elements with which the learners can exchange information and resources, so as to identify the internal operation principles, and maintain its ecological balance.

Thirdly, optimizing foreign language learners' cyber-based ecological environment requires continuous energy conversion and information transmission between learning activities and technological learning environment. The construction and optimization of an ecological cyber-based environment for foreign language learners needs continuous conversion of its energy and transmission of its information between learning activities and technological learning environment. Both learning activities and technological learning environment should develop with mutual interactions and restraints. Therefore, the optimization of technological learning environment must ensure that the environment functions with good learning interactions, intuitive and friendly interface design, as well as individualized curriculum setup which can fully reflect students' personalities. Considerations should also be given to the bringing up of students' practical abilities, especially listening and speaking skills with regard to students' different starting points and different levels. It is hoped that this can guide the students with success to carry out an individualized way of learning, and to meet their individual professional development needs.

Currently, the overall objective of college foreign language curriculum module is to train students' ability of comprehensive foreign language application, especially the quality level of listening and speaking abilities. At the same time, the curriculum module also aims to enable students to communicate with their future workmates and social partners effectively both in oral and written forms. Meanwhile, the objective also requires that students should train their ability to learn automatically and level up their comprehensive quality in response to the needs of China's social development and international communication. This further requires that students should get a further acquaintance of the purpose of foreign language learning, develop their ability to study automatically and cooperatively and obtain effective foreign language learning strategies, thus achieving qualified language proficiency.

Therefore, we can refer to this general objective when we are optimizing foreign language curriculum modules. The basic conditions for achieving this general objective are featured by five basic qualities, that is, language knowledge, language skills, learning strategies, cultural awareness and emotional attitudes. These qualities are relatively independent, but they have the same objective with close connection, interrelation and mutual support. On the whole, the combined system of foreign language curriculum module is the "chain" of learning ecosystem, reflecting the constraints and the balance of ecology. Among these qualities, language knowledge and language skills are necessary conditions for an integrated application of language competence, and for the understandings or absorption of cultural knowledge; learning strategies are not only the driving force for learning language knowledge and cultivating language skills, but also the prerequisites of developing self-learning competence; cultural awareness is one of the elements in language communication, as well as the rudder of idiomatic language application; emotional attitude is the internal momentum on the formation of students' reasonable values and their physical and mental development.

It can clearly be seen that the overall quality level and balanced development are the preconditions for the realization of curriculum objectives. The lack of any side or aspect would have a negative impact on optimizing curriculum module, thus affecting the optimization of the technological learning environment.

Fourthly, optimizing foreign language learners' cyber-based ecological environment requires a healthy emotional and psychological environment. During the cyber-based foreign language learning process, when community members interact with learning media, learning resources and other members of the same learning community, many subjective factors such as emotion and psychology will always be accompanied in the process. For learners, foreign language learning in the context of computers and networks not only involves learners' construction of knowledge and the process of cognitive growth, but also includes the emotional changes associated with the learner. This kind of emotional changes will directly affect the cognitive development of learners. Research shows that a good learning environment with good teaching resources can stimulate students' positive feelings and facilitate the conducting of intelligence activities and students' personal development. Therefore, a good emotional and psychological environment is a useful ecological factor in social ecological environment.

For example, it is necessary to stimulate and sustain students' motivation to learn when constructing and optimizing cyber-based ecological environment for foreign language learners. As the 21st century has witnessed the rapid development of computer networks, especially since the integration of networks into foreign language curriculum, students' learning mode and learning content have undergone profound changes. Network technology can change the students' thinking and behavior. On one hand, online education makes students' learning environment virtualized, so that students can play different roles in different network-based environments and can understand the different learning styles or lifestyles experienced by different learners; on the other hand, in computer-based or network-based classroom, the face-to-face communication between teachers and students or between students and students are no longer that direct and striking as it used to be, so the characteristics of students' learning, thinking, habits, etc. will more or less undergo subtle and profound changes under the new background.

Fifthly, optimizing foreign language learners' cyber-based ecological environment requires the combination of its common and special characteristics. The common features of cyber-based ecological environment refer to its systematic feature and dynamic balance while its special features are characterized by its openness, presupposition and dynamic generation. After optimization, the cyber-based ecological learning environment for foreign language learners should be an organic ecosystem as a whole. To be specific, the interactions between teachers and students, between students and students, as well as between students and computers should be in dynamic balance with sound development. The integration of computer networks into the curriculum requires not only learners' good interaction with teachers and other learners, but more importantly with computers and networks. Conclusively speaking, the ecological learning environment based on computer networks is just a small habitat existing in the educational environment. They both have common features of an ecological environment in essence and as a special artificial environment, each has its own unique features. It is necessary to combine the common and special characteristics in terms of the optimization of cyber-based ecological learning environment.

One of the main features within an ecosystem is its systematic feature which emphasizes interrelationships, interactions and functional unity between and of various elements in the ecological system. The normal functioning of cyber-based ecological environment for foreign language learners is based on interactions and mutual influences of the four sub-environments—physical learning environment, resourceful learning environment, technological learning environment and emotional learning environment, thus with systematic feature. The key point of systematic feature lies in the principle that a system's integrated function is greater than that of the sum of its all parts. Based on this, constructing and optimizing the foreign language learners' ecological environment requires good maintenance of its systematic feature which similarly ensures the interdependence of ecological factors of all kinds. Of course, this will bring the unity of its function exercised with those ecological factors. The ultimate goal is to achieve the optimal function of the entirely cyber-based ecological environment for foreign language learners and provide the best learning environment for them.

Next followed is the feature of dynamic balance. In a natural ecosystem, a dynamic and relative balance always exists between biological creatures and its living environment, as well as between different organisms and their populations. Consequently, the cyber-based ecological environment for foreign language learners should be constructed and optimized for its dynamic and relative balance which suggests that all ecological factors within the ecosystem should be highly adaptable in all aspects and the relationships between learners and their learning eco-environment or between various ecological factors should be highly coherent. As a result, the internal structure and external functions can be relatively stable. In brief, a good cyber-based ecological learning environment should be well-balanced, which can actualize the maximum exploitation of resources.

The openness of cyber-based ecological learning environment features in the exchanges of materials, energy, information and emotion with the external environment. The development and application of network technology and computer technology makes the cyber-based ecological learning environment a necessity. Network-based learners can break through the constraints in time and space. They can freely search for valuable information in cyber-based learning environment, no longer rigidly confining themselves to their geographical conditions.

Speaking of its presupposition, it refers to certain planning, anticipating and standardizing on constructing cyber-based ecological environment for foreign language learners, which indicates educators' intention, orientations and requirements. The cyber-based ecological learning environment being optimized is always developed and improved in the process of continuous designing, testing and modification. The hardware environment of learners needs ongoing maintenance in order to achieve a specific teaching or learning goal. The information ecological environment needs some kind of manual screening and processing in order to conduct smooth learning activities. The software environment needs to be upgraded and updated constantly. All these series of activities are on one hand intended to facilitate the optimization of students' learning eco-environment with computers and networks, and on the other hand to provide a more favorable environment for online learners or learning community.

Dynamic generation is related to the dynamic generation of foreign language learning and dynamic development of foreign language learners under the environment of computer networks. During the learning process, the ongoing interaction between the learning subjects and the series of learning activities experienced by learners can arouse learners' constant changes in emotional and cognitive psychology, making the learning process fraught with many uncertainties and dynamic tendencies. Only through the continuous and constant development and changes of the current cyber-based ecological environment for foreign language learners and the consistency between the learning eco-environment and the uncertainties of the dynamic learning process can learners have more enthusiasm for learning as well as more confidence in learning and more momentum in motivations. Therefore, it is safe to conclude that the dynamic generation of cyber-based ecological environment for foreign language learners is not only adaptable to the dynamic development of learners, but also contributory to positive changes of learners' knowledge, skills and emotional attitudes or values. Meanwhile, in the cyber-based ecological learning environment, learning subjects gradually form an integrated cognition and comprehension of the nature, society, selves, and even culture based on the newly generated cognitive, understanding and practical experiences through conversations, interactions, experiences and feelings. The whole process can be regarded as a generating process.

The cyber-based ecological environment for foreign language learners can be seen as a subsystem of foreign language education ecosystem. On the one hand, the foreign language education ecosystem keeps an input of technology, equipment, personnel, etc. which covers the following flows: material flow of capital, knowledge, etc.; energy flow and the curriculum, software, courseware, etc.; and information flow into cyber-based ecological system; on the other hand, the cyber-based ecological learning environment maintains an output of all kinds of information, where materials and energy cannot be directly imported but information itself can be converted into the wealth of knowledge which indirectly inputs materials and energy into social ecosystem.

The cyber-based learning activities from an ecological perspective are relatively integrated and sustainable with overall coordination. The main features of foreign language learning are to be seen in overall harmonious, dynamic balance and far-ranging connection. The overall harmony specifically involves all kinds of balanced interactions among various elements inside and outside the learning ecosystem while dynamic balance is manifested in a constantly developing and changing process of learning. Finally, far-ranging connection is shown by correlations of ecological factors or flows within the ecosystem and eco-learning environment.

For these ecological factors, they are unremittingly interrelated and inter-influenced during the entire learning process of cyber-based environment. It should be said that the optimization requires not only a growth in the number, but also an improvement in structure optimization and efficiency promotion, as well as a qualitative breakthrough. In short, in the background of educational system, the maintenance of dynamic balance in physical learning environment, resourceful learning environment, technological learning environment and emotional learning environment can subsequently expect continuous, stable and healthy development of foreign language learning.

◆ 4.2 ◆
Fundamental Principles for Its Optimization

Since the 20th century, more and more worldwide ecological phenomena show that the ecological system comprised by humans, environment and other organisms as well as the balance within the ecological system are essential to human beings' survival and development. The study on ecology featured by ecological phenomena and its laws has become more and more heated. Ecological theories also widely and deeply penetrated into the studies on other relevant disciplines. Through the research conducted on foreign language learners' learning efficiency by making comparisons both of their learning efficiencies before and after the ecological environment being optimized, it is found that ecological concepts such as ecosystem, ecological balance, ecological niche can be borrowed to optimize the current imbalanced cyber-based ecological environment for foreign language learners. The study of optimization can be conducted from the macroscopic ecological level and microscopic ecological level.

Likewise, the foreign language learning environment on the basis of computer networks is a typical educational environment, which is similar to the natural ecosystem with the characteristics of integrity, complexity, diversity and conscious activity. Ecology attaches great importance to the influence of environment on biological creatures. Based on this, this dissertation attempts to optimize the imbalanced learning environment by relating to principles of ecology in order to ensure that foreign language learners can more effectively and efficiently complete learning tasks. The main optimization principles are listed as follows.

4.2.1 General and Integrated Effect

The organic theory of ecology holds that the world is of a diversified unification, namely, within an ecological system, between organisms and the environment, among different communities, great mutual accommodation and highly harmonious integrity can be achieved via energy flow, material circulation and information interchange. Integrity comes as the primary feature. It tells us that without integrated connection and structure, it is impossible for the system to be in full function. A system as a whole should have its internal structure, and anything outside that structure belongs to the external environment, generally called environment. The system's influence on environment is called effect. The integrated effect of any system equals to the total amount of the combined effects of all parts within the system plus the structural effects coming about as the result of the interaction among the parts. The equation is E（Integrity）=$\sum$E（Parts）+$\sum$E（Interaction）. When $\sum$E（Interaction）>0, then E（Integrity）> $\sum$E（Parts）. In other words, when the integrated effect is larger than the effects of all parts combined together, it proves that the integrated structure produces interactive effect.

This idea inspires us to think that, when trying to construct or optimize the cyber-based ecological environment for foreign language learners, not only should we consider the educational effect of each sub-environment, but also give more efforts to analyze the structural educational effects resulting from interactions among the sub-environments. When $\sum$E（Interaction）<0, then E（Integrity） < $\sum$E（Parts）, that is to say, when the integrated effect is smaller than the effects of all parts combined together, it suggests that the structure is counterproductive, and this is rather common in society. Likewise, during the construction of a certain environment for foreign language learners, a phenomenon like that might happen, in other words, if in the process, the sub-environments are not made to interact harmoniously, they might become mutually exclusive, and mutually inferential. Finally, the educational effects of individual systems would counteract each other, such as the material flow versus the emotional flow, information flow against the energy flow. This well explains the existence of minus effect of the whole. Therefore, without the four independent but mutual relevant sub-environments, there would not be the integrated computer-based ecological system for foreign language learners; without the natural, scientific and effective interaction among these sub-environments, there would be nothing of a harmoniously, scientifically and fully functioning whole of a scientific structure.

The ecological view pursues integrity and harmony for the reason that our world is both atomic and integrated. Atomic refers to distinctions of species while integrity being the basic feature of the organic world. Reflecting on the computer-based eco-learning under the guidance of integrated effect principle, the author finds that, eco-learning should also follow certain principles, which can be put as follows:

Firstly, all the interactive elements involved in a learning process constitute an organic integrity;

Secondly, the objective of integrated eco-learning is to guarantee learners' natural and sustainable development in a general organic environment, where physical environment, resourceful environment, technological environment and emotion environment interact mutually, as an integrity.

Thirdly, the content of eco-learning is an organic integrity as well, to integrate information and technology into foreign language curriculum, taking on the feature of diversification. To integrate the learning content from multiple perspectives is an important characteristic of eco-learning.

The parameters and variables of every part within a system have a function of mutual adjustment and restriction, which produces an integrated effect. In the ecological environment for foreign language learners, all the ecological elements are restricting and related to each other. If you take one of them, you'll break the integrated balance. Hence, in order to optimize the ecological learning environment, we should establish an integrated ecological view, connecting sub-environments with ecological elements to bring the integrated effect into force.

Under a computer-based background, learning activity falls into a group symbiosis pattern of poly-directional interaction, cooperation and communication. Learners are not only producers of learning resources but consumers. The optimized eco-learning environment covers learning community, environment and all other elements within the learning system. The optimized integrity helps to realize the functions of certain learning activity and knowledge transformation. The four ecological sub-environments for learning, i.e., physical environment for learning, resourceful environment for learning, technological environment for learning and emotional environment for learning, are integrated into the overall ecological learning environment. Perhaps it may be said that the eco-environment for foreign language learning is just the sum of all sub-environments. Ecologically speaking, the functions of the four sub-environments are especially important, and the reason lies in the fact that the integrated effect of the optimized environment exceeds the integrated effect of its four sub-environments.

4.2.2 Principle of Niche Emphasis

R. H. Whittaker（1970）pointed out that in a community each species has its own corresponding position, of time or of space, different from the position of other species, and also has a functional position in biological community. The specific space-time positioning of each element within the ecosystem determines its unique form of adaptation and proper behavior, including its overlapping and competition, compression and release, separation and movement etc. According to the principles of ecological niche, if each factor in foreign language learners' ecological environment has a most suitable positioning of time and space for its survival, it shows that each of these elements has the right and dynamic niche, which indicates possible achievement of harmony with the environment.

Therefore, when it comes to the optimization of the imbalanced ecological learning environment for foreign language learners, we should give full consideration to the ecological niche of each factor within the ecosystem. Reasonable arrangements and planning of all sorts of resources should be made. The role of mutual supplement and reinforcement should be fully played among individuals, community and the ecological system which also have a different niche on their own. The integration of computer and networks into foreign language curriculum naturally defines modern information technology as the new ecological factor of foreign language learning environment. For this situation, the niches of elements such as students, the environment, methods, and means have changed accordingly. The elements of the traditional learning environment must have good interactions with the new added element—information technology through mutual adaptation and coordinated development so that each ecological factor can identify its appropriate positioning, i.e., finding out specific and reasonable niche for each element. For example, due to the introduction of information technology into foreign language environment, students have become the key "species", being the main ecological niche, while teachers, teaching administrators and technical staff act as the secondary main ecological niche. For each ecological factor, the exercise of their unique function and behavior leads the entire learning environment towards dynamic balance.

4.2.3 Degree of Resistance

Shelford（1911）put forward with the principle of degree of resistance. He held the view that the existence of a creature and its successful survival would inevitably depend on various complex conditions. If human beings purposely wanted to put a creature in danger of its extinction, the easy step was just to change any of the ecological factors within the system and make it beyond its due resistance. In a higher education system, no matter it is an ecological individual or ecological community or ecological system, in a certain stage of natural development, all has its upper limits and lower limits of adaptation （the degree of resistance） toward surrounding ecological environment and various ecological factors. Within upper limits and lower limits, which means at the most appropriate state, the main body can develop well. The degree of resistance is measured on different scales according to different colleges and universities, different people, different environments and different stages of individuals' physical and psychological development.

In cyber-based ecological learning environment for foreign language learners, almost every aspect, no matter it is the construction of physical learning environment, resourceful learning environment, technological learning environment, emotional learning environment or the main body in education system, is more or less related to the degree of resistance and principle of the most appropriate. For example, if the modern information technology, as the new environment ecological factor, is not controlled within the upper limit or the lower limit when functioning, it will result in the rejection against other factors and eventually lead to a paralysis of the entire environment.

Based on this principle, when optimizing the cyber-based ecological environment for foreign language learners, it is necessary to take into consideration the upper and lower limits of environmental factors for proper development. For example, in resourceful learning environment, as for the designing of three-dimensional learning and setup of teaching software, designers should ponder upon the ecological environment they are in and all the possible ecological factors corresponding with teaching software. Each should be controlled within its adaptation scope with clear division of specific responsibilities.

For foreign language teachers, they should be responsible for the collecting, sorting and filtering of text, images, animation and video or audio-visual learning materials; for education experts, they should be responsible for the design and arrangement of the content from pedagogical and cognitive perspectives to ensure reasonable knowledge structure and appropriate degree of content difficulty, in line with the cognitive rules for a gradual understanding; for software development engineers, they should be responsible for improving the learning materials of text, images, animation, video and audio-visual online resources already selected by the teachers by using various techniques, helping teachers and experts put the ideas in vision into reality, rather than solely relying on one party. Three parties—teachers, education specialists and software developers jointly participate in the planning, designing, developing and producing of teaching and learning materials and software during the entire process. The task is completed by definite division of labor force, thus avoiding the overdoing of the material development and production. Overdoing caused by a certain ecological factor will result in deficiencies and defects of teaching or learning software and lead to the imbalance between learners' ecological learning and software making.

Therefore, the functioning of each element should be controlled within limits in a way that all ecological elements should "obey the rules" instead of being unrestricted. Another example is the optimization of the material learning environment. Whether it comes to the setup of the physical conditions on campus and in the classroom, or to the classroom size, or to the teaching content and the manning level of teaching administrators and technical staff, both the quality and quantity should be kept within the two principles of the degree of resistance and being the most appropriate, so as not to cause all kinds of imbalances. One more example is about the optimization of information technology module in the technological learning environment. The principles of the degree of resistance should be used to avoid foreign language learners' "overuse", "underuse" and "abuse" of information technology, making the ecological factor—information technology function within the "rule" to ensure that learners can fulfill high-quality learning tasks.

4.2.4 Principle of Expansion and Adaption

The principle of expansion and adaption refers to the fact that the development of any enterprise, region or sector has its own specific resources niche. Successful development demands good expansion of resources niche and requirement niche, so as to transform and adapt to the environment. Expansion without adaption lacks stability and flexibility of development; while adaption without expansion lacks speed and force.

Combined with foreign language learning, the implications can be interpreted as students' existing differences and diverse characteristics. For enterprises, good expansion of resources niche and requirement niche will lead to success. For educational environment, it requires that teachers should adopt changing methods according to students' different niches and diverse features. The so-called "teaching students according to their aptitude" is the thorough reflection of the principle of expansion and adaption. It is the case in optimizing the ecological environment for foreign language learners which demands that foreign language learners' differences in competence or talent should be fully considered, in addition to the emphasis on the diversity and richness of ecological learning. The requirement niche law is particularly of enlightening significance in optimizing physical learning environment and resourceful learning environment.

For instance, in light of the differences in foreign language learners, we should chew upon how many students a multimedia classroom can hold, what equipment and devices are suitable for collaborative learning, or which teaching resources cater for students' autonomous learning. Meanwhile, we should combine the application of resources and equipment with teaching objectives and students' actual differences to fully bring the function and effect of new learning mode into play. For the optimization of resourceful learning environment, the choice and design of foreign language learners' learning mode must meet the students' requirements niches. To be specific, the optimization requires the combination of students' actual competence with their level of cognitive development, such as the learners' personality, gender, age, culture, customs and others which are likely to be related with learning strategies or learning methods. Generally, students with lower level of foreign language competence tend to have low-level cognition of foreign language and rely more on teachers' lecture or show-how lessons of computer networks. For students with high-level foreign language competence, they are capable of autonomous learning and competitive interactive mode. Another typical point is that the design and production of learning resources also require the consideration of learners' niches because students are not only producers of learning resources but also consumers. First, learners need to be clear about their personal needs and then constantly strive to meet their needs. Learning materials should not only be consistent with learners' needs but also with the goals and objectives of foreign language curriculum, as well as being consistent with their learning software and online text materials which are used to promote or support their ecological learning. In a word, great importance to learners' needs should be attached. The designing of curriculum goals and its content should be based on investigations and demonstrations. An attention on new learning mode and learning strategies under the environment of modern information technology should be fully paid.

Under the background of computer networks, the richness of learning mainly refers to the diversity of learning content and the respect for students and their personalities. Ecological learning or eco-learning involves rich curriculum resources and learning resources, which defines curriculum as an educational experience instead of being confined to academic disciplines, materials and learning programs. Eco-learning covers either two aspects—transparent curriculum and potential curriculum or two levels—students' behavioral changes and inner feelings. An eco-learning process is always based on the respect for individuals' differences and the promotion of students' diversified development. The ecological learning will certainly help to create a healthy, open and harmonious emotional learning environment. We can say that the theory of requirement niches within the principle of expansion and adaption has certain reference value in optimizing emotional learning environment.

4.2.5 Flexible Adaptation and Development

The principle of adaptation and development in ecology refers to the relationship between man and nature, as well as two interrelated aspects during the ecological process. Their mutual relationship can be expressed as follows: the adaptation of human to nature is a prerequisite fundamental condition while the changes and development upon human to nature must be based on the adaptation. Any kind of development must regard adaptation as the key guide, and the purpose of development is targeting at a higher level of adaptation. Any kind of human-nature relationship under the guidance of ecological principles first and foremost is a kind of adaptation relationship. This is the most basic human survival principle. Besides, human-nature relationship is also a kind of relation of transformation-exploitation-development. And this is the ultimate principle of human existence.

In the process of optimizing cyber-based ecological environment for foreign language learners, we should obey the same rule, that is, to deal well with the relationship between adaptation and development. Here, "adaptation" mainly refers to the learners' adaptation to the four sub-environments as well as the adaptation among various elements within the system, especially the adaptation of the new element—modern information technology to other ecological elements in the system. However, "development" mainly refers to the development of the four ecological sub-environments for foreign language learning and learners' development of competence in terms of their adaptation to the computer-based or network-based foreign language learning eco-environment.

Therefore, to mention the construction and optimization of foreign language learners' cyber-based eco-environment, the first key point lies in "adaptation" to be based as the premise. Specifically the following two aspects are listed:

The first and foremost refers to learners' adaptation to the four sub-environments. As for the adaptation of main body—foreign language learners to the ecological environment is concerned about learners' respective adaptation to physical learning environment, resourceful learning environment, technological learning environment and emotional learning environment under the entire cyber-based ecological learning environment. Learning activities are first restrained and influenced by these four sub-environments because any imbalance of sub-environment is likely to cause learners' in-adaptation. As a result, learners' adaptation to physical learning environment, resourceful learning environment, technological learning environment and emotional learning environment is essential to the coordinated and unified development between learners and the four sub-environments. Such kind of adaptation undoubtedly should be active instead of being passive.

The next aspect is the adaptation between various elements within the ecosystem. Because of the integration of computer networks into foreign language curriculum, foreign language learners should pay much attention to the mutual adaptation between learning content, access to information and other factors during the learning process and more attention to the adaptation of learners to other learners and computers or networks. Currently, the direct cause of the imbalanced foreign language learning eco-environment is that the new element of information technology cannot yet be compatible with other elements within the learning system in spite of the integration of computer networks into foreign language curriculum. For instance, in order to achieve the mutual adaptation between learners and other elements, learners must in the first place learn to change the existing ways to establish a new mode of learning. Swiss psychologist Jean Piaget once pointed out that students' learning process included assimilation and conformance. Assimilation was that in the process of interactions between students and knowledge, learners would bring the newly acquired knowledge into their existing cognitive structures or behavior patterns. Conformance meant that the new knowledge couldn't successfully be assimilated by learners' existing cognitive structures or patterns of behavior, and that it could adjust the existing cognitive structures or behavioral patterns in order to get adapted to the acquisition of new knowledge.

The adaptations of learners between other learners and computers are mainly characterized by the handling of teacher-learner relationship, learner-learner relationship, and learner-computer relationship within the ecological environment. With the integration of computer networks into foreign language curriculum, students should redefine the roles of other learners, teachers and computer networks. To conduct better adaptations of teacher-learner relationship, learner-learner relationship, and learner-computer relationship to the integrated foreign language curriculum will mean a lot to successful interactions in the cyber-based ecological learning environment.

The functioning of cyber-based ecological environment for foreign language learners is on the basis of the realization of its adaptation to the external environment which provides important subsistence and development for ecological learning environment and the fulfillment of the mutual adaptation between various elements within the system. What needs to be pointed out is that such kind of adaptation is not rigid but flexible, or at a higher level. The adaptation can not just stop at the superficial level, but have its ultimate goal of targeting at the harmonious and healthy development of the entire learning eco-environment and its individuals.

4.2.6 Principle of Growth and Restraint

The principle of growth and restraint in ecology tells us that any ecosystem has some favorable factors leading its development and some restraint factors limiting its development; the scarcity of resources leads to competition and intergrowth mechanism within the system. The role of intergrowth is to improve the utilization efficiency of resources, enhance the system's autogenic vitality and make sustainable development attainable.

Under the cyber-based ecological environment for foreign language learners constructed by humans, the dominant factor is of guiding significance in designing ecological learning environment. The dominant factor in the ecosystem can play the role of both a commander and a controller. The presence of a dominant factor is helpful for balancing and coordinating the relationship among learners, learning companions, facilitators and management administrators, guiding the entire learning environment towards dynamic balance.

For example, in the optimization of the technological learning environment, the dominant factors are the curriculum modules and technical software modules. This is because in the background of computer networks, the best learning model for foreign learners is the compound model of learning and autonomous learning on the basis of computer networks. The cyber-based classroom learning requires a good design of curriculum module. As to the courseware production, it should arouse and stimulate students' thinking, imagination and thorough understanding as much as possible during the process of foreign language learning, rather than making students fall into pre-set patterns, ideas or logical clues of the classroom learning. The autonomous learning mode requires a perfect design of technical software modules which can be achieved by ensuring the stability of a computer platform, developing online learning and assessment software to easily record students' learning efficiency, etc. The optimization of this kind will greatly stimulate students' interest of online learning on their own and guide students to sink into effective network interactions, thus improving their self-learning efficiency.

In another example, when constructing and optimizing emotional and psychological learning environment, the focus is to change students' traditional concept of cognition, to render more emotional concern to learners' computer-based learning and to give full play to the exercise of both students' learning autonomy and facilitators' guidance. There are four levels of emotional interactions and three levels of cognitive interactions in learning community under the environment of computer networks. The four levels of emotional interactions are instinctive level, behavioral level, conversational level and reflective level while the three levels of cognitive interactions are interactive operation, information exchange and interaction with each other through the concept. The levels of these two types reciprocally influence to make cognition and emotion interact through the learning process, thereby gaining the rebalance of smooth emotional flow under cyber-based foreign language learning environment and promoting the capability of cyber learners and the development of their creative thinking.

4.3

Comparison of Two Cyber–based Foreign Language Learners' Environments: Before Optimization and After Optimization

4.3.1 The Learning Environment Before Optimization from the Perspective of Ecological Balance

The basic characteristics of the ecosystem include the structural diversity, system's complexity, energy's flowability, material's cycling, system's dynamics and self-regulation （Shang Yuchang, 2003: 195）. Ecological balance is the hypogyny concept of ecosystem and also the key part on the chain of ecosystem evolution. Ecological balance of ecosystem is far from the "still state" of a balance, that is, in specific conditions, within ecosystem, producers, consumers, decomposers as well as the environment stay in a steady state due to interdependence, mutual restraint, mutual adjustment and mutual adaptation （Huang Yuanzhen, 2007: 124）. In other words, the ecological balance of the ecosystem that has been formed and maintained at a steady state is a relatively dynamic balance, which is realized by relying on the contact and interaction between internal elements as well as between system and surrounding environment, through continuous regulation of the internal structure and function. The ecological balance of the ecosystem can be interpreted as follows: under certain circumstances, through the internal and external material, energy, information passage and exchange, the system achieves the mutual adaption, coordination and integration between internal organisms, between life and environment. To some degree, this system is capable of self-control, self-regulation and self-development. At the same time, it is integrated, open, connected, diverse, balanced and systematic.

Based on the foregoing, it can be known that the computer-network-based foreign language learners' ecological environment is an ecosystem. The learning subject, subject and environment interact with each other and depend on each other through material flow, energy flow, information passage, and emotional communication under certain conditions. The ecological balance of computer-network-based foreign language learning environment refers to the balanced state, in which during operation every element keeps self-regulation, remaining in a relative steady state and maintaining healthy development. In the balance, the flow of the material（physical learning environment）, energy（technological learning environment）, information（resourceful learning environment）and emotion（emotional learning environment）varies according to the environment. However, the input and output can reach a dynamic balance in the end.

From the perspective of ecology, ecological balance is the key condition of creating and maintaining a harmonious, dynamic, positive computer-network-based foreign language learning environment. However, at present, a number of problems arising in the learning environment have seriously damaged this balance, resulting in ecological imbalance, which mainly finds expression in the imbalance between input and output of the computer-network-based foreign language learning environment. This imbalance occurs to both the element flow and the flow of material, energy, information and emotion in each sub-environment. It appears mainly as follows:

Firstly, the imbalance of the elements flow in the sub-environment leads to the imbalance of a certain flow. For example, foreign language education management is a comprehensive flow from the central government to local education administration sectors and a large number of schools. But many schools are too weak in the execution of foreign language teaching reform or curriculum reform, with the actual level of management and monitoring efforts considerably lower than what is prescribed by Ministry of Education and other institutions, theory mismatching reality, causing serious imbalance of material flow. The availability rate of the network resources itself is too low. The network resource is not suitable for students' learning content and learning activities, consequently, only a relatively less amount can be used. Furthermore, students are not familiar with the environment and methods of resource acquisition. Reasons from both sides lead to the imbalance of input and output of information flow. The underuse, overuse and abuse of multimedia technology during foreign language teaching, as well as the technical restraints during the students' online learning are also on the list. Low-value use occurs when the language laboratories and multimedia classrooms are not made best use of, many of which are only used for teaching listening, seriously influencing the value realization of the multimedia; over-value means that teachers rely on the multimedia technology too much, without considering the actual teaching situation; abuse refers to the situation that the multimedia equipment and the cultivation of students' language skills do not match, and the use of the equipment and technology are unreasonably quantified. As the energy carrier of information resources, the technology module can not play the role of navigation, resulting in the imbalance of energy flow. Teachers do not organize the classroom teaching systematically, can not properly carry out multi-media teaching and can not control the enthusiasm of students. As a result, teachers and students are lack of emotional communication and interaction in the background of computer networks, causing the failure of emotional flow.

Secondly, at present, imbalance arises in the flow between material, energy, information and emotion of each sub-environment. For example, what the school administration authorities did misfits the reality in capital investment for foreign languages learning needs, management and maintenance of equipment as well as management responsibilities of multimedia facilities. Inadequate funding, the phenomenon of "vacant" equipment resources together with unclear management division of labor cause serious consequences: classroom management is inappropriate; equipment maintenance is untimely; the normal use of multi-media classrooms are influenced; new equipment does not have acceptance inspection guarantee mechanism; the normal operation of multi-media classroom is difficult to be guaranteed and some other problems. On the one hand, it will be an obstacle for students and teachers to use multimedia equipment; on the other hand, it will lead to the low social recognition of foreign language learning in computer-network-based environment. This is an imbalance between material flow, information flow as well as emotional flow. In the computer-network context, the learner is still unable to make good use of multimedia equipment, to give full play to learning potential and to realize the effective self-study and individualized learning. Computer is just an auxiliary tool, and students still rely on the blackboard and chalk to acquire knowledge. It is probably because there is a wide gap between the actual needs and software of computer's teaching and learning, such as the overloaded information amount, too decorative information, or poor interaction. Thus teachers and students can not get good technical support. "Three-dimensional" teaching material cannot live up to its name, which is of poor quality and cannot effectively improve students' comprehensive proficiency. This is because the curriculum module design is unreasonable. Furthermore, it did not take into account the differences and needs of students and did not carry out planning and design according to the reform of curriculum goals. Really suitable and well-targeted learning resources are not enough, and the resources utilization is low, due to the lack of both integration design for students' needs and integration of various media resources as well as effective guidance for students from teachers. The result is manifested as follows: learners lack positive learning enthusiasm because they cannot adapt to new modes of learning; their enthusiasm fades and their learning motivation is not strong because they cannot systematically carry out learning activities in the classroom as planned or the academic pressure is excessive, leading to the imbalances of learning motivation and learning strategy and unsatisfying fulfillment of human interaction, human-computer interaction and self-interaction. In short, rejection phenomenon appears between information flow and energy flow, and in the end results in the disorder of emotional flow.

Ecological balance is dynamic. Maintenance of ecological balance does not just mean maintaining their original steady state. In fact, ecological systems can establish a new balance with helpful human action, with a more reasonable structure, more efficient functions and higher ecological efficiency. Based on this, optimization can be conducted in the imbalanced ecological environment of foreign language learners, in the context of computer networks, to enable various elements to reestablish a new balance so that new dynamic balance of the whole environment can be maintained.

4.3.2   The Crucial Optimization Principle—Under Ecological Niche Principle to Construct a Harmonious, Dynamic and Flexible Environment

As we all know, in the context of network information technology, the cyber-based foreign language learners' ecological environment covers netlike ecological factors with interactions and interdependence, in which energy flow, material flow, information flow and emotional flow exist between these factors and ecological chains. At present, the emergence of various imbalances and disorders in the four sub-environments of the whole cyber-based environment will directly give rise to the abnormal functioning of learners' learning system and mutual exclusion in the flowing process of energy, material, information and emotion. The disturbances and disorders among various ecological factors lead to the so-called "tissue rejection", which will ultimately result in the loss of the entire environmental balance, even paralyzed. The so-called "tissue rejection" refers to the conflicts between the original learning system and other teaching factors, especially between the new element and other elements. Or rather, the new learning mode or other elements can not function effectively and actively in a new environment. In other words, since the new element—information technology which centers on computer networks was integrated into foreign language curriculum, "tissue rejection" occurs between the new environment and the original foreign language learning system. But how can we prevent such "rejection" and deal with these disorders or imbalances? The optimization of foreign language learners' environment must be carried out.

To optimize the computer-network-based learners' environment, it is a must to guarantee harmonious, natural and ecological niches so that the system elements such as students, the environment, methods, tools, information technology, etc. can interact with each other and have mutual adaptation, making the whole learning environment on its way to a dynamic balance. In addition, the optimization can also enable the interaction and coordinated development between information technology and other factors so as to advance the ecological and harmonious development of the integrated foreign language learning ecosystem. The achievement of the interaction and coordinated development requires, first and foremost, a specific, reasonable niche for each element in a learning environment, that is, to find out the proper positioning of each factor.

4.3.2.1 Niche from Micro Perspective

On the micro level, in the foreign language learners' environment, systemic elements include individuals, groups and group chains. Individuals mainly refer to students, teachers, teaching administrators and technical staff. Groups refer to the respective students' group, teachers, teaching administrators' group and technical group with different identities and experiences.

A group chain is divided into two levels: first, the chain comprises of information, knowledge, skills, learning, technology, methods, design, assessment, management, etc., while the second chain is composed of teachers, students, curriculum, teaching materials, equipment, networks, etc. The optimization of foreign language learners' ecological environment requires a best survival time and space position for each element of individuals, groups and group chains, so that each ecological element can function uniquely. In this foreign language learning environment, students are the key "species" thus in the main niche, while teachers, teaching administrators and technical staff are in secondary main ecological niches, who are the main producers of learning resources. Anyway, the four should cooperate with each other and enjoy dynamic coexistence.

Students' niche: students' computer competence should match computer's various functions. Or rather, computer networks should truly become an integral and indispensable part of the learning process, which requires more cooperative learning opportunities between learners and more discussions or exchanges between learners to complete learning tasks because the communication, interaction and exchanges between learners can add some vigor to their language learning environment and better encourage each other through healthy competition.

Teachers' niche: during the computer-based and network-based college English teaching process, teachers should pay attention to students' initiatives and enthusiasm to develop their autonomous learning ability. Teachers, from time to time, need to assign them tasks, to organize self-learning activities, and then check the results. Without this management part, students' self-learning efficiency will be greatly reduced because of their passiveness. So special attention should be paid to students' monitoring, supervision and encouragement, which is a crucial part in the process of their learning. In addition, the learning system is better stably maintained. Any kind of problems caused by the unstable computer system can severely affect students' enthusiasm for autonomous learning. As a result, problems like failures in logging in or starting the test system or voice recognition should be avoided at utmost, reducing the inconveniences of teaching management at the minimum level.

Teaching administrators' niche: the integration of computer and networks into foreign language curriculum tells teaching administrators that they should know how to make the system function well at all levels, make all elements well-coordinated and perfectly-matched. Teaching administrators should perfect the management and training mechanisms of teachers and strengthen the training and construction of college English teachers. The construction and upgrading of teachers can be achieved by enhancing teachers' training and conducting learning-and-experience sharing activities. For example, since the implementation of education reform, the author's school, through different channels, has taken a variety of ways to send college English teachers to go abroad for advanced studies on a regular basis, and to participate in various trainings of education reform, intercollegiate exchange, or research activities. These trainings and exchange activities will effectively promote the update of the college English teachers' teaching concept and their using of new teaching model and new teaching methods to help them master modern teaching methods to improve their teaching abilities. Teaching administrators possibly also strengthen the construction of college English academic teams, cultivate more academic leaders and excellent teachers, and actively organize teaching and research activities in order to comprehensively improve the overall quality of college English teachers, and promote the implementation of college English teaching reform. In spite of the complexity of teaching management which covers a wide range of aspects, an administrator must hold an integrated concept that it is necessary to give full play to different levels of regulatory agencies and functional departments, and fully arouse the enthusiasm and initiatives of teachers, students, and managing staff.

Technical staff's niche: the information of teaching equipment should be digitized so that the staff who are in charge of devices and techniques can more effectively deal with device management, facilitating the students' and teachers' use of the equipment, also making it easier for statistics and calculation of equipment workload and device failures. The establishment of networks should provide teachers with non-real-time equipment maintenance. For temporary and non-real-time problems such as installing software or borrowing certain equipment, network-based communication is needed not only for simple maintenance, but also to make teachers' choices varied. The network of teaching services in which all problems' processing has entered into the database can offer technical staff an opportunity to check the devices at any time or make statistical analysis of existing problems so as to get well prepared for future management and device processions.

4.3.2.2　Niche from Macro Perspective

On the macro level, the systemic elements of foreign language learning eco-environment include foreign language education policy, learning mode, students' self-management, information and learning resources, facilities for learning, and informationalized learning. The optimized foreign language learning eco-environment is reasonable and balanced which can flexibly coordinate the various elements' niches within the system to form a new systemic balance.

The optimization of foreign language education policy means that the documents issued by the Ministry of Education will further put an emphasis on the management of college foreign language education in local colleges and universities. The central institutes will more closely relate to the actual situation of local schools and push the administration staff in colleges and universities to have a better understanding of reform goals and objectives.

The optimization of students' learning emphasizes that students are the center in the learning process requires students' active initiatives, discovery and innovation to explore knowledge and demands the effective integration of students' autonomous learning and modern information technologies with computer networks as the core.

The environmental optimization also enables students to understand how to quickly and effectively obtain and store the needed information, know how to use modern information technology to solve problems, and deal well with the relationship between the "what to learn" and "how to learn". Specifically we can provide students with three effective modes of learning: problem-based mode of learning, network-based mode of inquiry learning, and resource-based mode of collaborative learning, individual learning, and scenario learning.

Students' self-management includes planning, monitoring and evaluation. The optimizing of students' self-management have three points: (1) to ensure that students can select their learning software according to their personal interest; (2) according to their comprehensive ability and their progress in learning, students can select different learning content of the same software learning, entirely at students' disposal; (3) actively guide learners to have a sense of self-management, especially the awareness of planning and strategies, and to get rid of the passive learning mode that students have been used to for a long time so that they can take the initiative to make arrangements for their own learning and become masters of learning.

The optimization of information and learning resources is to give full play to "guiding". The integration of computer networks into foreign language curriculum requires an organized and effective use of rich information and learning resources. The integration is based on network construction of information resources. In view of this, learners need to make full use of information organization and retrieval tools to quickly find out the relevant materials online and avoid the interference of large number of irrelevant content. Students can choose to study the needed learning resources from the huge amounts of data on the network and make order transformation of the out-of-order information, thus reducing the potential hazards of information "disorientation". Secondly, learners need to improve their self-understanding, enhance information-processing ability and judge competence, give full play to self-management skills and navigation capabilities, and enhance the learning efficiency.

When it comes to the optimization of learning facilities, colleges and universities will greatly enhance the basic administrative tasks of equipment and facilities, such as the purchase of new equipment, the elimination of discarded equipment or devices, and the management of existing equipment. The whole staff in charge of facilities is quite familiar with multimedia equipment and its operation. Colleges and universities will further enhance the construction of informationization and networking of computers, as well as the optimization and improvement of computer-network-based teaching platform in order to improve foreign language teaching and learning environment and provide hardware and technical support for the innovative teaching model.

As for informationalized learning, it should be of tolerance, initiative, innovation, openness, and interactivity. In other words, learners, with the support of information technology, need to actively interact with other learners, and construct a harmonious ecological environment to complete the learning tasks with high quality.

The second point is the establishment of conversational and collaborative learning mode supported by the educational technology. In the actual teaching process, more opportunities should be provided for conversational and collaborative learning. In the process of teaching design, students' practical environment should be constructed to increase the training of students' listening and speaking skills and to develop and explore students' communicative competence. Learners can communicate with each other on any network computer, without time and space limit or access restraint, fully making students' learning universal and open. The depth and breadth of issue discussions brings freeness and innovations to cyber-based learning.

4.3.3 Result After Optimization—An Integrated, Dynamic and Balanced Ecological Learning Environment

Based on the principle of niche, the optimization of foreign language learning eco-environment has achieved the rebalance of all the elements, changing the imbalanced environment into an integrated, dynamic and balanced ecological environment. The features of the optimized learning eco-environment are as follows: all elements are compatible with each other within the eco-environment and the relationships among various elements are easy to be regulated and coordinated; learning activities are constrained to a certain degree, with smooth interactions, interdependence, mutual conversions of all elements; the eco-environment has an impact on individuals' healthy development; the eco-environment can also promote cultural development. After optimization, material flow, information flow, energy flow and emotional flow have reached a high degree of mutual adaptation and harmonization, forming a new stable, compatible and harmonious ecosystem.

The optimized learning eco-environment is rich in its applications, compatible and harmonious, the four sub-environments being of harmony and compatibility too. As a result, the whole foreign language learning eco-environment is promoted to be on its way to be compatible, dynamic and healthy, in which the main constituent elements include the overall balanced physical learning environment, dynamic and compatible resourceful learning environment, flexible and convenient technological learning environment, as well as the harmonious and healthy emotional learning environment. The main constituent element also includes three coordinated interactions. The following is the detailed analysis of these ecological constituent elements.

4.3.3.1 Integrated and Balanced Physical Learning Environment

The optimized physical learning environment tends to be a balance one. Either from top level or local level, from macro level or to micro level, all institutions truly implement the relevant provisions or principles issued by the Ministry of Education and other higher institutions. The leading panel in colleges and universities will strengthen its awareness, make clear and reasonable arrangements of task assignment, and make concerted efforts to organize hardware, software and human resources to standardize the management and establish a scientific and perfect management system for technology and equipment just to keep abreast of information trends in the teaching process. In a word, the all-round guarantee of the modernization and technicalization of foreign language education does a lot good to the overall coordination between ecological factors with the entire education system and brings great benefits to the maximum efficiency of various elements in the optimized ecosystem.

4.3.3.2 Dynamic and Compatible Resourceful Learning Environment

A dynamic and compatible resourceful learning environment is the essence of a harmonious foreign language learners' ecological environment. After optimization, in the resource-based learning eco-environment, the sustainable development of learners' learning objectives can be realized. The ecologization of learning content can be brought into effect. The multi-dimensionalization of learning channels can be achieved. The ecological evaluation of learning efficiency can come true. All elements within the eco-environment are in mutual adaptation and interdependence, as well as in co-operative and matching relationship. Information technology is harmoniously compatible with the foreign language curriculum, that is to say, the new ecological element—information technology is successfully integrated into resourceful learning eco-environment. Information technology and other elements enjoy good co-operation and integration, thus maintaining the stability and balance of the entire resource-based learning eco-environment.

4.3.3.3 Technological Learning Environment with "One Basis"+ "One Focus"+ "Two Supporters"

Through optimization, in technological learning eco-environment, the curriculum module, software technology module, information technology module and teaching technology module will establish a good navigation system respectively. Each module can fully play the role of navigation. The design of each module can not only stimulate learners' interest in learning, but also facilitate learners' free jumps in the learning process according to their learning progress they have made. Among these modules, curriculum module is the basis or foundation; teaching technology module is the focus or main body, while software technology module and information technology module act as two supporters or aides. All the modules are mutually overlapping and converting, forming a flexible, convenient, economical and efficient three-dimensional system. In short, after optimization, in technological learning eco-environment, the four dominant modules, namely the curriculum module, software technology module, information technology module and teaching technology module interact though differences and competition exist, and will ultimately promote learners' effective learning within the ecological environment of technology.

4.3.3.4 Harmonious and Healthy Emotional Environment

The optimized emotional learning eco-environment is generally harmonious, healthy and happy with mutual assistance, in which students' cognitive operations are effectively improved and learning efficiency is greatly enhanced under the guidance of positive emotions. After optimization, learners will realize that the information technology can be used as both a cognitive tool and an emotional tool for motivation to promote their autonomous learning, with a purpose of giving full play to their initiative, motivation and creativity in their learning process and truly becoming the main body of information processing and the knowledge-oriented teaching object. In an environment where students can explore their knowledge independently, conduct mutual interactions on a multi-level basis, learn collaboratively, and share all available resources, the foreign language learners will undoubtedly get themselves involved in the interactions with their teachers, other learners and computers and networks. In addition, their mutual respect, harmonious communication and mutual cooperation will result in a positive and harmonious learning environment. Emotional behaviors like positive emotional guidance from teachers and teachers' assist in students' correct attribution will gain on-going concern from relevant sectors in society, that is to say, improve the social recognition of cyber-based foreign language learners. Likewise, social institutions will in reverse offer their support in terms of learning services and other types of services in order to encourage foreign language learners to learn and develop sustainably under the computer-network-based ecological environment.

Only in an environment abundant in relaxation, maximum appropriateness and warmth can a personalized, self-oriented, user-friendly and open learning model be established for students' continuous and healthy development.

4.3.4 Conclusion: the Model of Cyber-based Dynamic and Balanced Foreign Language Learners' Ecological Environment

All in all, the four sub-environments, after optimization, can in deed realize the informationlization of foreign language and vice versa. In other words, on one hand, the information technology is integrated into foreign language curriculum by the greatest extent. Computers and networks are fully applied to students' learning and teachers' teaching. On the other hand, the information technology is embodied by foreign language curriculum. The optimization, to a maximum degree, develops students' awareness and interest of foreign language learning in the background of information technology. As a result, students can freely deal with any kind of problems cropping up in foreign language learning process with informationalized methods. The four sub-environments can enjoy interdependence, interaction, mutual adaptation and harmonization, and constitute the entire dynamic balance of the ecological environment of foreign language learners（As is shown in Figure 2.1 below）.

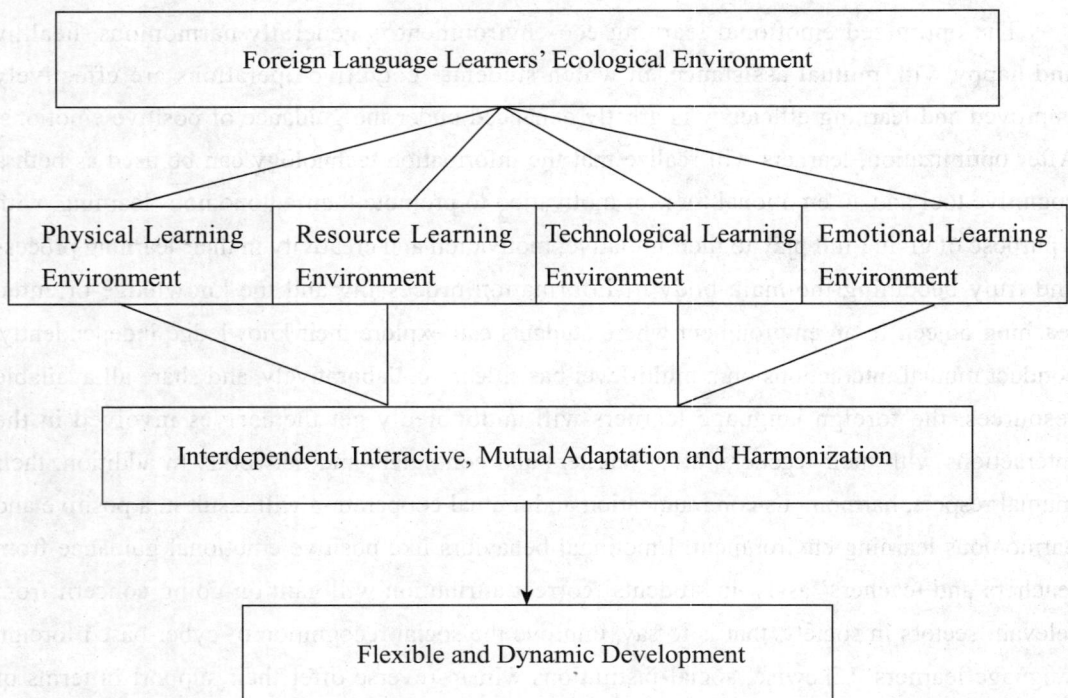

```
                Foreign Language Learners' Ecological Environment

  Physical Learning    Resource Learning    Technological Learning    Emotional Learning
  Environment          Environment          Environment               Environment

        Interdependent, Interactive, Mutual Adaptation and Harmonization

                        Flexible and Dynamic Development
```

Table 4.1   Dynamic & Balanced Foreign Language Learners' Ecological Environment

4.4

Ecological Reflections on Foreign Language Learners' Environment

In the first place, environment is a system, which means that it is an integrated whole made up by various parts, structures, levels and environment. Foreign language learners' environment is formed by many interrelated and interacted parts（elements）according to certain hierarchy and composition, and it has specific functions. Therefore, it is a system. In the whole system of foreign language learners' environment, every part（element）has a specific function; however, the general function of the system is greater than the summation of every element's function. Apart from system theoretical approach, based on the concept of the ecosystem, the foreign language learners' environment is also a kind of ecosystem. It is a natural and open ecological whole formed by every learning element and environment in certain space, in which every necessary element, during their existence process, competes with each other, interacts with each other, depends on each other and accordingly shapes a healthy and orderly state.

According to ecological point of view, no life organism can exist isolated. Any organism must rely on the surrounding environment and can only exist by the exchange of material, energy and information with the surrounding environment. Just as plants' growth need soil, sun, water, air and nutrients, the language ability acquisition process of foreign language learners must be finished in certain ecological environment, which provides a meaningful place for foreign language learners' language input and language output as well as decides the interaction of various elements of learning, such as learners' learning objectives, learning content, learning methods, forms of learning, learning time, learning materials.

Study should be conducted about how foreign language learners got access to effective learning with teachers, administrators, learning mode, information technology, methods and means, other learners and surrounding environment. The ecosystem of foreign language learners is a learning function whole formed by foreign language learners and their learning environment. In the system, learning environment, learners and teachers, other learners as well as other groups are closely related to each other and interacting with each other. Efficient learning is achieved by the input, absorption, output and feedback of language knowledge. It is a dynamic balance system and accordingly the foreign language learners' ecosystem can obtain natural and harmonious development.

4.5

Importance of Optimizing Cyber-based Learning Environment

The optimization of ecological environment for foreign language learners under computer-network background is a practical subject with realistic significance by itself. It firstly depicts an overall outlook and aesthetic style of an ecological school; then, it restricts the elaboration of internal elements within the ecological learning environment.

The computer-network-based ecological learning environment itself is an ecological system. Building a harmonious computer-network-based ecological environment for foreign language learners is crucial for sustainable development of foreign language education. The computer-network-based ecological learning environment for foreign language learners complies with the trend of integrating network information technology into foreign language curriculum. It is a basic principle that the construction of an ecological environment for foreign language learners can not be developed separately because it should be connected with the viewpoint of an entire ecological environment. Such being the case, the construction of the four sub-environments must be set as the key focus to accelerate the improvement of an integrated ecological learning environment.

From the theoretical perspective, optimizing computer-network-based ecological environment for foreign language learners is a kind of questioning on the integration of computer networks into foreign language curriculum. Before optimization, the connection between systematic factors was separated in foreign language learners' learning environment. Ecological theory implies the birth of a new research angle which focuses on harmonious coexistence of man and nature and aims at a sustainable development. Research on ecological study environment is a research turnover that corresponds with this new research perspective, i.e., to view the learning activities as a special ecological system and dialyze co-effectiveness and operation mechanism in between various elements of foreign language learners' learning environment. And all above have certain value and significance to the expansion of topic-based study fields. The integrity, connection and harmonious coexistence of learning activities, as mentioned in this dissertation, will also have certain implications and significance on enriching and developing teaching and learning theories.

From the practical perspective, foreign language education in China is facing a new round of reform. The new curriculum reform advocates active interaction and common development with students during the teaching and learning process. It also focuses on students' initiatives and independency, pays attentions to inspiring students' learning interest so that every student can be fully on its way to healthy development. The author believes all these are the necessary steps towards an ecological learning. The present study will also help teachers and students have deeper reflections on class teaching and learning by using the views of integrity, connection, harmonious co-existence and dynamic development, so as to expand study activities ecologically and luster teaching and learning activities to bloom with ecological glory.

4.5.1 Effective Means to Improve Learners' Learning Efficiency

Since the introduction of modern information technology into foreign language curriculum, many students have encountered the refection of foreign language learning because of the changes in the use of technology, learning mode, learning materials etc., thus forming a vicious circulation. By optimizing the cyber-based ecological environment for foreign language learners, students can not only clarify internal relationships between the new element and other elements within the ecosystem, but also find out his proper niche.

In a harmonious and pleasant learning environment with sustainable development, learners can quickly adapt themselves to the new computer-network-based classroom teaching mode and extra-curricular self-learning mode. The optimized environment can stimulate students' interest in learning English to a large extent.

Under the background of computers and networks, if learners want to improve learning efficiency, the use of advanced technologies like multimedia and networks become a must to construct an ecological learning environment with high quality. Foreign language learning is a complex system. Learning efficiency is affected by many factors, such as the learning environment, age, gender, motivation, linguistics competence, personality, learning strategies, emotional factors and so forth.

The newly added factor, i.e., computer networks, is an important element which has an impact on foreign language learning. Language learning environment, as a special kind of social environment, is a complex and integrated system consisting of a variety of elements; it is also a complete system comprised by people, objects, things, time, space, etc. The effectiveness of its functioning is closely related to teaching activities, directly affecting the quality of learning activities and processes. The introduction of computers and networks particularly requires the construction and optimization of the current foreign language learning environment in order to achieve the complete optimization of resources and improve students' foreign language proficiency and learners' learning efficiency.

4.5.2 Important Means to Construct a Harmonious Campus

Compared with the entire social ecosystem, a school is just an ecological point. The reasonable arrangements for this ecological point can not only provide students with a good learning environment, but also cultivate students' sentiments and stimulate their interest or motivation in learning. Campus environment generally includes the school's hardware environment, all kinds of teaching and non-teaching activities, and the overall learning atmosphere and so on. The development of information technology and abundance of network resources both offer a good platform of establishing personalized learning space for students' personalized learning. The integration of educational technology which is multimedia-based and network-based into the modern foreign language classroom further calls for the construction of a harmonious, healthy and dynamic ecological environment for foreign language learners. Only by doing so can we make full use of campus media and online teaching resources. Only in this way can we extensively conduct a variety of "second class activities" and provide students with more opportunities to train their foreign language skills. Only by doing so can we establish good academic atmosphere for language learning, which will ultimately help students to set up and maintain a good attitude towards learning, expand students' individual learning space, and achieve harmony between people and the campus.

By optimizing the cyber-based ecological environment for foreign language learners, students no longer exclude the introduction of the new element. They still believe they are studying in an open and free learning environment. In the learning process they can take the initiative and consciously make good use of external resources and conditions. They can construct their own learning environment. They can correctly handle the interactive relationships between them and their corresponding teachers and computers. They can search for knowledge autonomously, learn collaboratively and cooperatively, share online resources and carry out various learning activities in a positive and harmonious ecological environment with mutual respect, harmonious communication and mutual cooperation.

4.5.3 Crucial Guarantee to Maintain Learners' "Best Niche"

In the optimized cyber-based ecological environment for foreign language learners, the school personnel will keep in mind the concept of diversified talents, respect for individual choices, encouragement in personal development and advocate of students' sustainable development. Therefore, students' learning should also take on its diversity. Niche theory, as a theoretical tool to examine social phenomena and problems, can also be used to view the diversity of students. Niche theory offers a new perspective to strengthen the learners' self-awareness in individual differences and recognition of diversified development, i.e., to ensure the students' most appropriate niche.

Under the environment of computers and networks, the designers who are in charge of the designing of curriculum, software, resources, and technology development should be dedicated to students' natural being, social being, and harmonious development of autonomous creation. The designers should also focus on the unity of individuals' needs and social needs, the unity of diversity and integration, as well as the unity of foreign language learning environment and sub-environments, encouraging students to move towards a comprehensive, free, harmonious and healthy development. The interrelationship between learners and cyber-based ecological environment is an integral and essential aspect of educational process. The integration-based foreign language learning should be that students understand the niche of each factor in ecological environment, such as the proper niche of information technology, learning methods, learning strategies, network resources. In addition, students know well what kind of ecological factors will hinder their learning and personal development, and what kind of ecological factors will promote their development and growth.

4.5.4 Essential Foundation to Keep Harmonious Coexistence of Teachers and Students

Ecological theory tells us that the world is diverse and each individual has its own uniqueness. Either an individual as opposed to other individuals, or a single group, compared with other groups, is a "dissident". However, the "dissidence" is the original nature of the diversified world, and the differences between different elements within the system sometimes can promote the development of another element. The optimization of the cyber-based ecological environment for foreign language learners can help in a general establishment of a harmonious, dynamic and positive teacher-student relationship on the basis of mutual understandings. Teachers will show their acknowledgement of students' initiatives and dynamism, while the students can actively and dynamically get involved in the learning process. The teacher-learner relationship is always in the formation of a dynamic process, following the ecological operating mechanism of being balanced-imbalance-rebalanced. The ecological teacher-learner relationship is dynamic and formative.

In the optimized cyber-based ecological environment for foreign language learners, the teacher-learner relationship is established in the interactions between teachers and learners and in their mutual exchanges. In other words, teacher-learner relationship is not naturally produced, but a generating process and a creative process. Teacher-learner relationship is generally speaking a kind of two-way and interactive influence. The interactions and influences between teachers and learners are not just one-time or intermittent but a chain and a continuous loop process. It is in such a continuous and dynamic process that teachers and students are involved in constant interactions and mutual influences.

4.5.5 Continual Momentum to Ensure Sustainable Development of Ecological Class

The ecological theory has provided a new way of thinking for foreign language classroom study. The foreign language classroom which targets at developing students' "communicative competence", with "active teaching" as the teaching mode and with "cooperative learning" as the means of foreign language studying, will undoubtedly contribute to interactive teaching and the creation of an ecological classroom. The optimized cyber-based ecological environment for foreign language learners is an important guarantee for constructing such an ecological classroom because in the optimized learning environment, students, the main body of foreign language classroom, will lay great emphasis on the multi-dimensional interactions between other students and teachers with the support of computer networks and other multimedia equipment. This ecological foreign language classroom is a dynamic and open process from beginning to end where students and teachers promote and complement each other so that the "group dynamics" of a class is to be played and ultimately improving learners' overall foreign language competence.

Therefore, the optimization of cyber-based ecological learning environment for foreign language learners and the study of an ecological class from ecological perspective are not only the requirement imposed by foreign language curriculum reform but also the specific purpose aimed by foreign language teaching and learning. The discussion of inherent relationship between cyber-based ecological learning environment for foreign language learners and classroom teaching or learning is of great help in fundamentally solving the current problems existing in college foreign language teaching. The discussion will provide constructive implications for optimizing the ecological structure of a foreign language classroom ecosystem, helping balance various ecological factors within the system and establishing an ecological classroom with harmonious and sustainable development.

5 Chapter

Empirical Investigations on Constructing and Optimizing Cyber-based Foreign Language Learners' Ecological Environment

5.1

Research Background

The current research, under the guidance of theoretical framework, is targeting at the following contents: physical learning environment, resourceful learning environment, technological learning environment and emotional learning environment, college students' actual use of computer networks in English class, the students' positioning of teachers' role, students' role and computers' role, the present situation of college students' autonomous learning under the background of multimedia networks, whether the basic skill training of computers can improve students' performance in cyber-based listening test, the test of effective degrees in instant feedback towards error correction, and questionnaire surveys on the test of in-class activities.

The design of the questionnaire has comparatively high requirements. First of all, questionnaires are designed by teachers with rich teaching experience, trying to cover a range of topic-based questionnaires. Secondly, questionnaires are done based on numerous relevant documents, and a comprehensive and meticulous study of existing literature.

The questionnaire is evaluated with five scales of LIKERT involving physical learning environment, resourceful learning environment, technological learning environment and emotional learning environment. Students are required to fill in Arabic numerals in the column of "Choices" according to their actual conditions （5 points: complete conformity; 4 points: over 50% conformity; 3 points: 50% conformity; 2 points: below 50%; 1 point: basically disconformity）. According to the provisions of the five LIKERT scale, the value of the statistics averages 3.0. The version of statistical tools adopted is SPSS 11.0 academy package.

The questionnaire on the "actual use of computer networks in college English classrooms" is in the form of multiple choices: the five LIKERT scales are done as to teachers' role, students' role and the role of computers. Students can rank the arranged numbers according to their own ideas or experiences: the number "1" means that it is absolutely not important; 2 means that it is basically not important; 3 means that it is important occasionally; 4 means that it is basically important while 5 means that it is very important.

Under the background of multimedia networks, five LIKERT scales are used to find out the present situation of college students' autonomous English learning. Students are required to choose the proper one in the column of "choices" according to their actual conditions. (complete conformity; 4 points: over 50% conformity; 3 points: 50% conformity; 2 points: below 50%; 1 point: basically disconformity)

People often regard that an instant feedback of an error correction is very effective. However, would this feedback make students more nervous and let them make more mistakes? To answer this, three different computer tests are given, each test with two parts. When the students are doing the first test, we are sitting by them. Whenever the students make a mistake, we immediately stop him and correct it. In the second test, we still sit down beside students. If they make mistakes, the teacher nearby will help them correct them later. In the third test, we let students finish the test independently, and then tell them the wrong part. Every second part of the test will be finished by students independently. Each exercise will include 10 parts where they might make a mistake. The best grade is 0, and the poorest is 10. If the student got 10 points, it signified ten mistakes that student made. These results will be used as the research data. We aim to test whether there are significant differences between the three tests. If differences exist, then where do these differences lie?

In the present study, exam papers are also used to evaluate students' improvement on their scores. The evaluation standards are unified and the papers are checked by research members forming an assembly line. Academy SPSS 17.0 packages are used to make comparison between the two grades.

The examination test 1: in order to find out whether students' training of basic computer skills will influence their results of listening tests under the background of multimedia platform, class A (59 students in total) from Qiongzhou University were chosen. First of all, divide class A into two groups randomly: group A and group B. Students in group A do not receive any basic skills of computers in multimedia classroom and students in group B have received the training. A comparative analysis will be conducted in terms of their respective listening test scores to find out the research result.

The examination test 2: experiment 1 conducted in September 2010 in Qiongzhou University targets at 30 English majors of 2009 randomly selected. They all come from Hainan Province, having been learning English for 7 years. All having passed the college entrance exam, we can assume that their English level is comparatively consistent. Based on this, another entrance test for comprehensive English is arranged. Experiment 2 is the same class who has 4 hours' comprehensive English learning weekly in multimedia network with three-dimensional teaching materials. Their performances of final exams in comprehensive English will be studied, on the premise of the supposition that the difficulty degree of both their entrance examination and final exam papers are in conformability.

5.2
Method

The main research methodology in this study is based on macro research method, and other research methods such as literature review, statistical analysis, and case study are all adopted in order to prove the appropriateness and preciseness of some micro viewpoints and basic structures.

5.3
Object and Content

5.3.1 Object

Five teachers in the investigation project worked in Qiongzhou University, Sanya, Hainan for one semester, during which they carried out investigation activities, such as questionnaires, informal discussions and English test with over 300 college students with different majors.

5.3.2 Content

The contents of investigation involve eight aspects of cyber-based foreign language learning.

1）The influence of physical environment on college students' English learning;

2）The influence of resourceful environment on college students' English learning;

3）The influence of technological environment on college students' English learning;

4）The influence of emotional environment factors on college students' English learning;

5）Students' respective positioning towards the role of teachers, students and computers;

6）The actual state of utilizing computer networks in college students' English class;

7）The current situation of college students' autonomous learning under the cyber-based background;

8）Comparison between imbalanced and optimized cyber-based ecological environment for English learners by SPSS.

5.4
Design and Procedure

By making both qualitative and quantitative data analysis, the author conducted an experimental study to verify the foreign language learners' use of computer networks, ecological imbalance and the necessity of the environmental optimization. Aiming at an effective research, the author randomly chose a class in Qiongzhou University as an experimental class. Firstly, the students were surveyed on their learning interests, learning strategies, learning environment, learning methods, learning goals, learning tools, learning attitudes and learning motivations both under the background of multi-media networks and without the multi-media network environment. It intends to reflect their current situation of English study and provides possible foundations for the research. Then the in-class students were equipped with computer networks for one semester. In the end of the semester, a final test was held. After one semester of learning, the test scores of this experimental class with the two different backgrounds are significantly different. This means that the external factors and internal factors under the background of multimedia networks as well as the English learners' learning strategies, learning methods and learning tools have formed a dynamic ecosystem with an interactional interdependent relationship. Through this dynamic system, the students can gain more significant achievements by autonomous English learning. The construction of an ecological environment for foreign language learners under the background of multimedia networks stresses a close, harmonious, dynamic and balanced ecological coordination relationship between learners and their learning environment, which ensures the sustainable development of foreign language learners.

5.5

Quantitative Data Analysis on Investigation Result

5.5.1 Research Result

5.5.1.1 Physical Environment Factors Influencing Learners in Learning English

In order to generalize college students' physical learning environment for foreign language learning, the author designed a related questionnaire with twenty-eight questions. Correspondingly, 40 students from Qiongzhou University were surveyed randomly. The author took back 35 questionnaires, and took 30 of them as samples to analyze. The questionnaire is clearly set out in the appendix, while the investigation result is shown below.

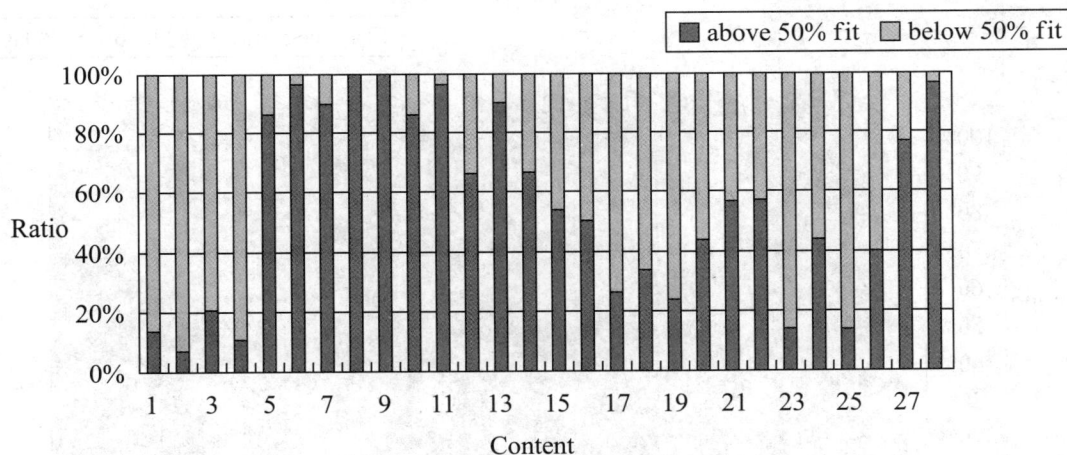

Graph 5.1   Students' Physical Learning Environment

According to Graph 5.1, we can draw the following conclusions:

Only 10% of them think there is a book store on and around their campus. 87% them find that there are many mobile vendors around their campus, and 97% of them are exposed to the long-term construction on campus. Meanwhile, 90% of their living quarters are around the playground. When they are having classes in cyber-based classrooms with projecting camera, 33% of students couldn't see the screen clearly yet if they took a back seat, and also there are 53% of students who have already experienced the computer's broken sound system, freezes, breakdowns or even crashes. Half of the students have computers at home, and 73% of them are equipped with networks throughout the year. The main online activities are browsing gossip news, playing games, chatting, shopping, and watching soap operas or movies, listening to the songs and writing blogs. Among them, main activities of 43% of students are chatting and shopping; 57% of students prefer to watch American soap operas or movies, and the same percent of students are crazy about listening to English songs online, while only 13% of them are managing their blogs. Only 13% of them know the state-issued policy about the construction of cyber-based three-dimensional teaching system, and 60% of students believe that the school has not well implemented the policy of National English Teaching Reform.

5.5.1.2　Resourceful Environment Factors Influencing Learners in Learning English

In order to better understand college students' resourceful learning environment for English learning, the author designed a related questionnaire with 20 questions. Correspondingly, 40 students from Qiongzhou University were surveyed randomly. The author took back 35 questionnaires, and took 30 of them as samples to analyze. The questionnaire is clearly set out in the appendix, while the investigation result is below.

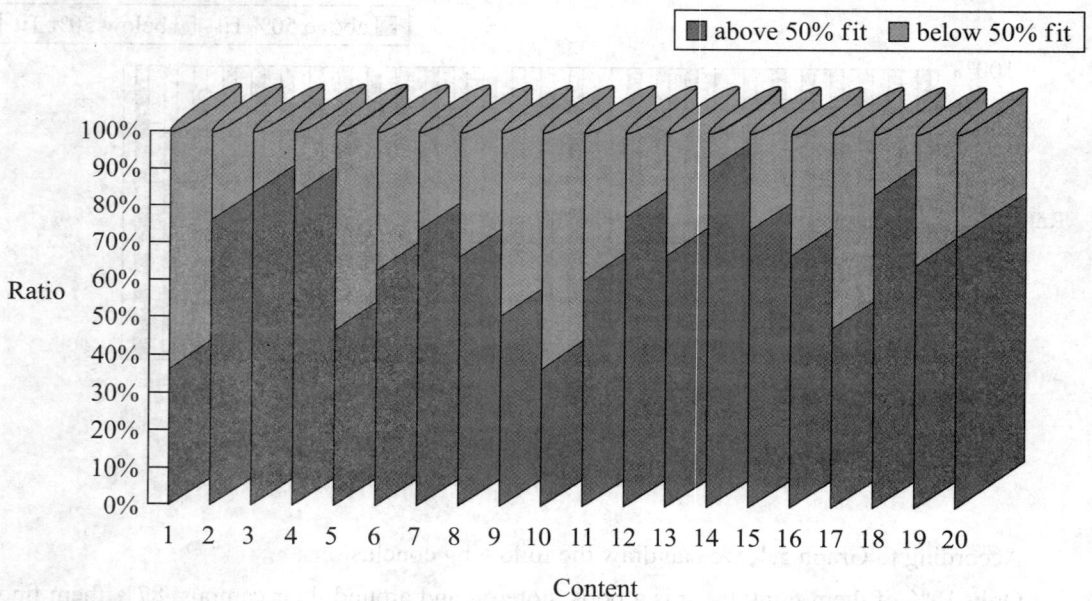

Graph 5.2　Students' Resourceful Learning Environment

The above graph shows the following conclusions:

Comparing to the multi-media teaching models, 37% of them are still accustomed to the traditional blackboard-chalk teaching model, and 77% of them get into the habit of taking notes while listening to the lectures. 47% of them are majoring in English just for the sake of a college degree, not out of their motivated interest. Therefore, 63% of students spend much more time practicing the CET-4 and CET-6 in order to get certificates in English. Actually, 33% of students don't have any plan for English learning, and just half of the students can take advantage of the CD-ROM in English textbook. However, only 37% of them could finish the entire English learning materials in each semester. With regard to teachers' courseware, 67% of students feel that the courseware is filled with words, while 47% consider the courseware is pictures-occupied; 63% of them complain that the teacher spends too much time illustrating the details of courseware and 70% think that the teacher spends too much time explaining the details of courseware.

5.5.1.3   Technology Environment Factors Influencing Learners in Learning English

In order to get a good knowledge of college students' technological learning environment for English learning, the author designed a related questionnaire with 15 questions. Correspondingly, 35 students from Qiongzhou University were surveyed randomly. The author took back 30 questionnaires, and took them as samples to analyze. The questionnaire is clearly set out in the appendix, while the investigation result is below.

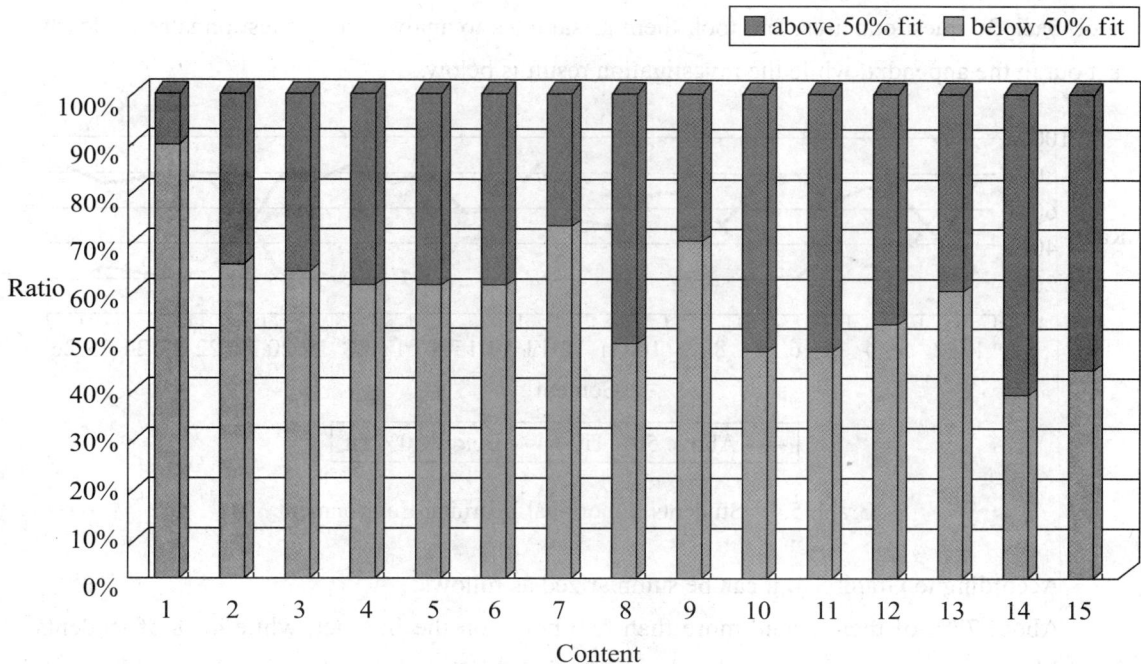

Graph 5.3   Students' Technical Learning Environment

By analyzing Graph 5.3, the following statements can be obtained:

60% of them think that the overloaded information in class results in the flood of invalid information. The same percent of students are the victims of "no pubic class without multimedia" on campus. Also 60% of students find that the function of multi-media equipments in school is no other than a projecting camera. After handing out all the questions to the students in class, the teacher is disposed to apply "referential keys". For this, 73% of students have shown their common consent. Half of the students think the pictures, sounds and animation in teachers' courseware would distract their attention from the important content. There are 53% of students respectively complaining that using the computer-based learning platform not only takes much more time, but also fails to instantly monitor students' online activities such as chatting, movie watching. This is obviously off students' learning tracks. About 60% of students consider that the amount of teaching information is beyond their depth, leading to their "informational disorientation". At the same time, 60% of students don't know how to deal with the "massive" network information.

5.5.1.4 Emotional Environment Factors Influencing Learners in Learning English

In order to get well acquainted with college students' emotional learning environment for English learning, the author designed a related questionnaire with 26 questions. Correspondingly, 35 students from Qiongzhou University were surveyed randomly. The author took back 30 questionnaires, and took them as samples to analyze. The questionnaire is clearly set out in the appendix, while the investigation result is below.

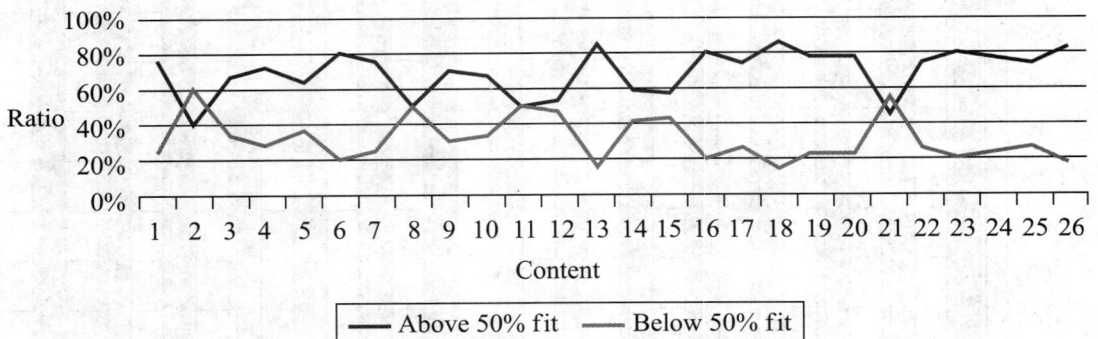

Graph 5.4　Students' Emotional Learning Environment

According to Graph 5.4, it can be summarized as follows:

About 77% of them spend more than two hours on the Internet, while 40% of students spend less than one hour surfing the net. 33% of students feel that they can reasonably make use of study resources on the Internet while 76% of the surveyed students think that English scores will negatively influence their enthusiasm for learning. Half of the students think it is shameful not knowing how to use the computer while 70% of students think that the frequent use of multimedia is not good to one's eyesight. When it comes to the application of computer-based English learning in class, 67% of students find the English exercise difficult, and 53% of them consider the English learning tasks are with too much pressure. Meanwhile, 50% of students think that multimedia-based English learning will easily lead to a lack of regular study plans, and 60% of students feel that it will reduce the interactive communication among classmates. At the same time, 87% of students think that they are far away from teachers' direct guidance and 71% of them feel that they can't receive their teachers' timely feedbacks in multimedia class.

5.5.2 Analysis of Investigation Results

5.5.2.1 The Imbalance of Physical Learning Environment

Foreign language learners' physical learning environment includes natural environment and social environment. Some schools are located in downtown areas, with very poor surroundings and campus conditions. Moreover, there is always big noise, little fresh air and insufficient sunshine in classrooms, dorms, libraries and labs. Although Ministry of Education encouraged colleges and universities to establish self-learning centers with cyber-based environment, yet quite a lot of places cannot afford the computers or technological equipments due to the lack of funds, hence no available networks. For some colleges and universities, though there are good supports for computer networks, the coordination between school administration for networks and teaching faculty is not good, teachers do not have the final say on computer rooms, resulting in the imbalance between teaching process and teaching management. Although some students can have access to network, too many disturbances confound students' effective learning. In current physical learning environment, imbalances also exist between national education policy and local institutions' implementations of the policy. The diagram below is the actual situation of utilizing computer networks in college students' English class. It can be found that 63% of students make frequent use of the network, while 37% of them occasionally use it.

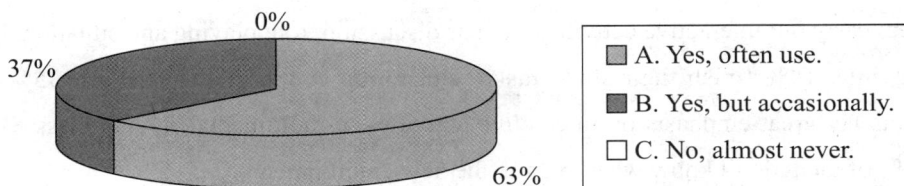

Graph 5.5   The Practical State of Utilizing the Computer Networks in College Students' English Class

5.5.2.2　The Imbalance of Resourceful Learning Environment

Resourceful learning environment includes those learning factors, such as learning mode, teaching materials, lesson plans, reference materials, books, web resources. Imbalances of resourceful learning environment mean that most schools use three-dimensional text materials while the teachers are still using the traditional teacher-centered pedagogy in which the teaching concepts, methods, tools, and teaching assessment are all very traditional. What's worse, there are quite a number of teachers who hold the view that regular foreign language teaching can be without the use of computer networks, and that it is a waste of time on computer-based teaching preparation and a great burden on computer-based teaching. In a word, the current situation is in great contrast with what Ms. Wu Qidi （former vice minister of Ministry of Education） proposed at the video conference on trial implementation of college English teaching reform in 2004. She mentioned that "the reform of current teaching mode is to change the traditional model characterized by teacher-textbook-chalk, student-blackboard as well as teacher-teaching, student-listening into an active and personalized learning mode featured by the integrated combination of computer networks, teaching software and class."

Some teachers understand some advanced teaching theories, such as constructivism learning theory or philosophy of student-centered and so on, but they don't put them into practice. Or the quality and attainment of some teachers can't follow the step of development. Or few teachers hold enough confidence in the application of information technology. The above ones are far from the reform requirement of foreign language teaching.

This kind of teaching disorder causes the imbalance of learning environment. The learning mode is still lecture-based, not an initiative one. Graph 5.6 shows the main activities in cyber-based English classroom. On the one hand, 27% of them get used to the reference of teaching courseware, listening to the lecture and taking notes. At the same time, 22% of them prefer the practice of English words and translation between English and Chinese, and main activities of 8% of students are centering around CET-4 or CET-6. To sum up, 57% of them are still doing certain traditional non-reciprocal activities in multimedia English class. On the other hand, 21% of them carry out interactive activities such as discussion, role playing and situational dialogues; meanwhile, 14% finish their study tasks with group cooperation. In short, 35% of college students lay great emphasis on interactive activities in multimedia English class. Besides, the rest 8% of them don't know what to do in the new environment.

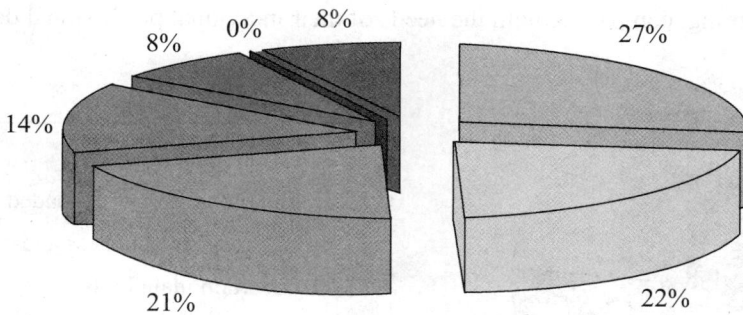

8% 0% 8% 27%
8%
14%
21% 22%

A. refrence of teaching courseware, listening to teachers' lectures, taking notes
B. words practice, English-Chinese translation
C. discussion, role playing and situational dialogues
D. group cooperation
E. doing CET–4 or CET–6 papers
F. don't know what to do
G. others

Graph 5.6   The Main Activities in Cyber-based English Classroom

5.5.2.3   The Imbalance of Technological Learning Environment

Technological learning environment means that during the learning process, learners can freely choose learning theories and have a good support system with suitable interface design, thus to stimulate learners' interest in learning and to ensure each functional module to be well guided by the system. Technological learning environment can not only facilitate learners' free jumps if they feel it necessary during the learning process, but also provide good opportunities for students' group discussion and collaborative learning. But currently, in many colleges and universities, the design of functional modules are not made according to students' differences, i.e., the modules do not fully reflect the individuality or take students' different levels into account, neither improving low-level learners' foreign language competence nor creating opportunities for high-level learners' further development. This can be seen as the imbalance of technological learning environment. The ideal and balanced technological learning environment is one which can not only consolidate students' language foundations, but also help cultivate and develop their practical abilities, especially listening and speaking abilities. The balanced technological learning environment is one which can not only guarantee the stable improvement of students' foreign language proficiency, but also be of great help in students' independent and individualized learning, compatible with the needs of their individual professional development.

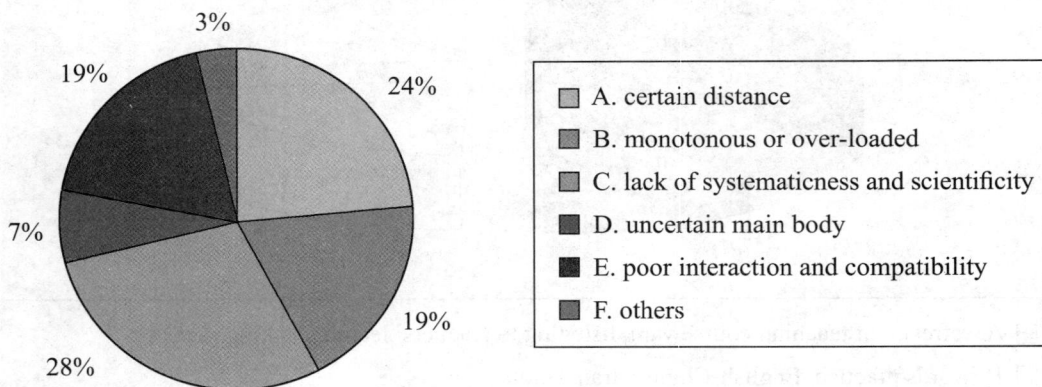

Graph 5.7   The Main Problems of Teaching Courseware in Cyber-based English Class

Graph 5.7 clearly shows the following points:

When it comes to the cyber-based English learning, 28% of the students consider that the biggest problem of teaching software lies in the fact that network materials are just simple listings and combination, lack of systematicness and scientificity. This point can keep the teachers aware of knowledge coherence, systematicness and scientificity when they are developing and making teaching courseware. From the graph, we also know that 24% of them think that there is still certain distance between teaching courseware and actual teaching requirements, which requires teachers' sense of specific teaching needs. In addition, 19% of them feel that the information in teaching courseware is either monotonous or over-loaded, and the same portion of students believe that there is poor interaction and compatibility of the teaching courseware, which is very difficult to be re-edited.

Meanwhile, in most colleges and universities, the abuse of multimedia has been a big issue under the compute-network-based environment. Regardless of the actual teaching needs, a variety of media are used blindly, resulting in the flooding of class information and the excess of invalid class information, which will both disperse students' attention and affect the achievement of teaching goals rather than support foreign language teaching. Even in some schools, the situation that "where there is multimedia, there is a class" is quite common. However, the so-called "multimedia courseware" is only simple words plus some pictures, which can be easily shown by a projector. It is undoubtedly a misuse of good technology for minor purposes and a waste of resources. The due value of computers and networks is unfulfilled. Multimedia has become veritably "superfluous".

In addition, the overloaded information has resulted in "disorientation" phenomenon which refers to the proposition that if human brain receives excessive information in a short time, it comes to a standstill. It is one the advantages of computers to store large amounts of information. But some of our teachers overuse the computer technology when producing the courseware. For example, they exhaustively list all the detailed and trivial content but have to speed up the information transmission due to limited class periods. The only result is that students are forced to be surrounded by dazzling multimedia information, unable to encode and decode the due knowledge, which directly affects the students' understanding and mastery of its due content and meaning. This is "disorientation" under the cyber-based learning environment.

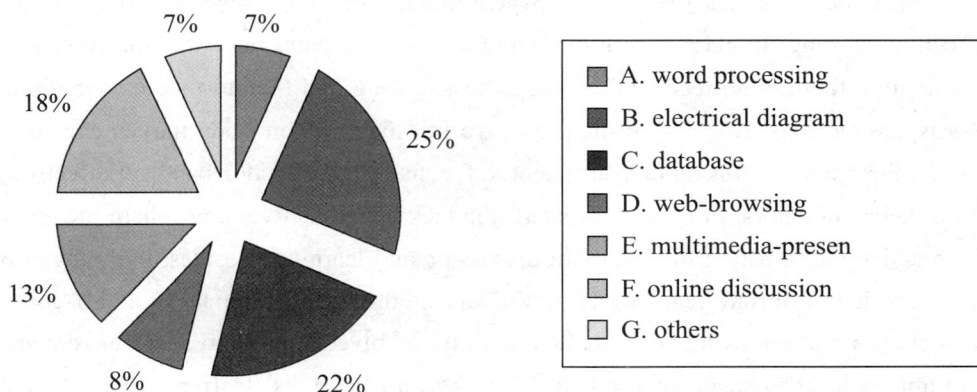

Graph 5.8   The Technology Problems the Students Meet When They Use
the Cyber-based Computer for English Learning

The teaching materials are not designed in accordance with individuals' specific requirements. The low utility ratio of textbooks, reference materials and network resources results in plenty of waste. What's more, English learners can't make full use of web resources for not having received regular training. Graph 5.8 tells us the technological problems the students meet when they are using the computer for English learning. 25% of them think the major problem is how to deal with the electrical diagram, while 22% of them find the operation procedures of database difficult. Besides, 18% of surveyed students find that the use of online discussion tools is the main hard part to crack, and 13% of them can't go along well with the presentation of multimedia. In addition, only 8% consider web-browsing as a block, and 7% of them regard word-processing as the main technological problem. Generally speaking, 65% of them are acquainted with the very basic operation of computer networks; however, their operation level just rests on the superficial level, which needs to be greatly enhanced.

5.5.2.4   The Imbalance of Emotional Learning Environment

The emotional learning environment consists of three parts: psychological factors, interpersonal interaction, and social recognition of learners. Psychological factors include learners' cognition, affective learning, learning attitude, learning methods, learning concepts, self-control in learning, etc.; the success of interpersonal interaction （including self-interaction） plays a considerable role in learners' self-learning; the adoption of learning strategies and learning methods has a direct impact on learners' learning effect and on social recognitions of learners.

Psychological factors: learners in learning community are separated in time and space, leading to greater distances among learners' emotional exchanges. The current cyber-based teaching concept is lack of learners' psychological feelings which directly affects learners' effective learning. In classes with the integration of computer networks into foreign language curriculum, there is no teachers' enthusiastic lecturing and face-to-face explanation. In other words, for teachers, it is very difficult to give full play to their body movements and polished charm. For students, it is quite insufficient to feel teachers' affections and get effective guidance from their facilitators. For the class itself, the lack of interactive atmosphere prevents students from active participation in classroom discussion and learning. Besides, the integration causes students' inappropriate learning concepts and methods and their lack of self-control in the new environment, making students unable to be involved in effective and passionate learning and unable to keep sustainable attention, all because learners' learning concepts, motivation, emotion, and other psychological factors impose great influence on learning interest and initiative, as well as on good maintenance of learning time and learning effect. In the computer-network-based environment, the imbalance of psychological factors directly affects learners' cognitive development.

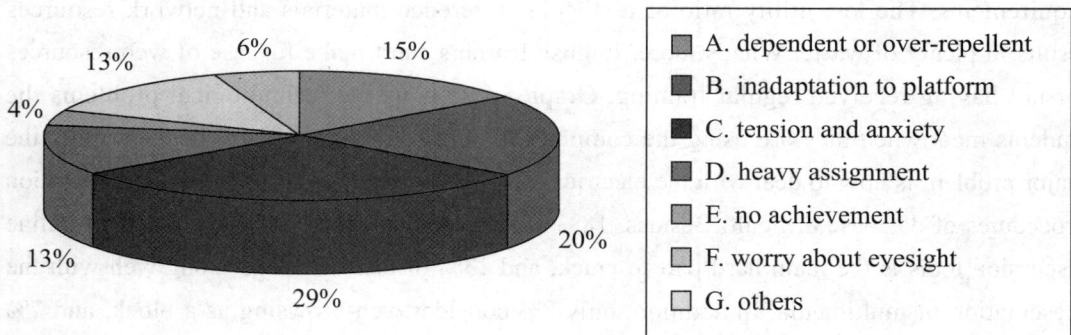

Graph 5.9   The Current Emotion in Cyber-based English Classroom

Graph 5.9 tells us the current emotional existence in cyber-based English classroom. 29% of them feel the study tension and anxiety brought by the new learning mode. 20% of them are sick of study because of their inadaptation to cyber-based course platform. 15% of them find themselves too much dependent on or over-repellent to computer networks. What's more, 13% of them think the school assignments are so heavy that they have a sense of frustration. Another

13% of them are worried about their eyesight.

Interpersonal interactions: the computer-network-based foreign language learning involves continual interactions between learners and learning environment. But since the integration of computer networks into foreign language curriculum, interactions between learners and computers and among learners themselves are not fully achieved. That is to say, the exchanges and sharing of information are not basically realized, which is a failure in learner-learner interactions; learners can not deal well with a variety of network tools and technologies to access learning materials and to acquire knowledge, which is a failure in learner-computer interaction; learners do not have a deep and thorough understanding of the content and are unable to make the gained new knowledge integrated with the existing cognitive structures, which is a failure in self-interaction.

Social recognition: "College English Curriculum Requirements" clearly stipulates that the design of college English curriculum should take advanced information technology into account, in order to promote the computer-network-based foreign language teaching, to provide students with good language learning environment and conditions. However, the actual situation is not what is expected. On the contrary, imbalances emerge known as the so-called "disconnection" between "central requirement" and "local implementation". In other words, many colleges and universities do not fully implement the new requirements for the curriculum. For example, there are still many problems in the construction and operation maintenance of computer networks in cyber-based learning environment, leading to the lack of good interactions among learners, the lack of a vigorous and dynamic learning environment, and the poor positioning of computer-network-based foreign language learning. In a word, there is low learning efficiency for learners in computer-network-based foreign language learning environment, which has inevitably and seriously hampered social recognitions of cyber-based foreign language learning. Or, it is safe to say that the fundamental reason for "poor social recognition or acceptance" is that the output of computer networks (the quality of foreign language learning) is inconsistent with the investment in constructions of computer networks.

As is discussed above, the four learning environments—physical learning environment, resourceful learning environment, technological learning environment and emotional learning environment, or the so-called sub-environments of computer-network-based foreign language learning environments, are seriously imbalanced, which can be concluded as follows. The learning modes, concepts, learning methods, learning content, learning media, etc. are incompatible with existing cyber-based learning conditions, teaching faculty, sources of students, management quality, and matching materials; learners' social environment, regulatory mechanisms, management, emotional and psychological factors, etc. are all more or less in disorder. These imbalances or disorders undoubtedly have brought about an imbalanced information-technology-based learning environment, impossible to survive in the school education system. These serious imbalances further indicate that it is extremely urgent to find out a new approach to reexaminine the underlying causes and take effective measures. Therefore, it is unlikely to make it by relying solely on traditional foreign language teaching and learning theories because the occurrence of imbalances has been a great challenge to these traditional theories.

◆ 5.6 ◆
Empirical Investigation of Foreign Language Learning in Optimized Cyber-based Ecological Environment

5.6.1 Optimized Physical Ecological Environment Improving Learning

Firstly, as the physical learning environment is the basic condition for foreign language learners in cyber-based environment, the optimizing of physical learning ecological environment is the primary factor to promote students' learning environment. By optimizing, leaders or principals, who are in charge of colleges and universities, should not only pay more attention to the investment and building of school hardware, but also actively take corresponding measures in concrete details to implement superior macro-policies. Besides, they need to optimize the construction of teaching resources and learning software for foreign language study, and to optimize the management, purchase and safeguarding of facilities. What's more, they should optimize the layout of multi-media language laboratories and classrooms, and zealously make full use of campus network. For example, the classroom should keep light on and maintain proper temperature. As for the layout of campus, first and foremost, they should guarantee the accessibility of campus networks, and secondly guarantee the coverage of green plants to create a relaxing learning environment. Or rather, the leaders and principals could raise funds in various ways to expand the investment for education technology, to aggrandize teaching and learning equipments, to further promote the efficiency of classroom teaching, and finally to push forward the real ecology of foreign language learning in the context of information technology. Each teacher should realize the necessity and urgency of strict implementation of modern education by definite goals and effective managements. Only by doing so can the improvement of college teaching quality be ensured. Besides, regular or irregular training of computer technologies for teachers, administrative staff and technicians should be conducted in an all-round way. The training can take various forms of advanced studies, lectures, contest, etc. In order to find out whether this kind of training on computer operations will have an impact on the improvement of learners' dictation scores in cyber-based multi-media class, the research team took 59 students from the same class in Qiongzhou University as samples. Firstly, the team was divided into two groups randomly. Group A with 30 students did not receive any education of computer operation in multi-media classroom while group B of 29 students were trained.

Table 5.1.1 Check if computer training has significant influence on scores

Research Hypothesis	Computer basic operation training has no significant influence on students' dictation scores.
Significance Level	.05
1-or 2- tailed	2-tailed
Research Design	
Dependent Variable	Dictation Scores
Measurement	Interval
Independent Variable	Group
Measurement	Nominal
Independent or Repeated-measured	Independent
Statistical Procedure	T-test

By analyzing the data in the appendix with SPSS 16.0, our research team got Table 5.1.2 below. The result（t=-4.396, p<.001）tells us that there is significant difference between the students who received basic training of computer operation and those who did not.

Table 5.1.2 The result of whether training on computer basic operation will have an influence on the improvement of learners' dictation

		Levene's Test for Equality of Variances		T-test for Equality of Means				
		F	Sig.	T	Df	Sig. (2-tailed)	Mean Difference	Std. Error Difference
Data	Equal Variances Assumed	.259	.613	-4.396	57	.000	-11.57414	2.63309
	Equal Variances Not Assumed			-4.381	54.288	.000	-11.57414	2.64171

In a word, it means that the basic training of computer will affect the improvement of listening scores for foreign language learners.

It also shows that the optimization of the integration of information technology influences the scores made by foreign language learners.

5.6.2 Optimized Resourceful Ecological Environment Improving Learning

In the first place, facing the immense knowledge and ever-updated network information, foreign language learners' learning mode is featured by flexible ways of teaching, mechanization of learning places, diversification of learning content, informatization of learning process, and diversity of learning standard. With the support of computer networks and other multi-media, learners effectively and flexibly obtain a kind of individual, independent and heuristic study by autonomous options, reasonable reception, scientific processing and timely feedback. This kind of learning mode is much more about autonomous study, cooperative study and explorative study, with passive reception in face-to-face lectures being the supplement; therefore, it can finally cultivate learners' ability of how-to-learn, life-long learning and updating of knowledge structure. It is a learning mode with sustainable development. Learners pay attention to multi-dimensional interaction with teachers and other learners, showing that it is consecutively a dynamic and open process.

In order to give a better instruction for foreign language teaching, the research team ask 15 English majors in Qiongzhou University to rank the effect of the following ten class activities: group competition, group discussion, writing composition, dictation training, grammar drills, class quiz, answering questions, vocabulary drills, watching English movies and imitating mini-TV drama. These ten activities are all optimized teaching methods. The investigators use SPSS 16.0 to find out whether the students have shared opinions on the effect of these ten class activities. The original data can be seen in the appendix. The research design is below:

Table 5.2.1   Check if there is no agreement among the Ss in activities used in class

Research Hypothesis	There is no agreement among the Ss as to the relative merit of the different activities used in class.
Significance Level	.05
1-or 2- tailed	2-tailed
Design	
Measurement	Ordinal
Statistical Procedure	The Kendall's Coefficient of concordance

Table 5.2.2   The result of whether there is a significant relation among the students as to the relative merit of the ten different activities used in class

Test Statistics

N	15
Kendall's W^a	.404
Chi-square	54.568
Df	9
Asymp. Sig.	.000

a. Kendall's Coefficient of Concordance

The analysis in Table 5.2.2 reveals a significant relation among the students as to the relative merit of these ten activities used in class（p=.000<.01）. So we reject the Hoc, and the correlation of agreement is .404, which means that these ten optimized class activities get a high acceptance among the students. In other words, it shows that the optimized multi-media English environment is harmonious.

In the second place, through optimizing the imbalanced resourceful learning environment, students' learning and teachers' teaching form a good dynamic circle. To be specific, all the teachers and learners could use network technologies to digitize the teaching and learning content. With teachers' assistance, students can not only reach a high academic level but also be equipped with knowledge and skills in information technology. And the evaluation for learning effect could also promote the exploitation and application of new information technology. The compatibility stresses the fusion and integration of various resources to ensure the harmony between information technology and learning links. In other words, we should regard information technology which is the core of computer networks as the cognitive tool for students' autonomous learning. Besides, we should also apply 3D textbooks, reference materials, papery textbooks and various network resources to foreign language learning process, in order to make a mutually coordinated and reciprocal relation among all sorts of learning resources and links. It is necessary for both English teachers and technicians of computer software to design a practical and effective English teaching courseware closely associated with students' actual level as well as the different characteristics of different orientations.

The next is an experiment conducted in resourceful learning environment. The research team randomly select a class of 30 English majors in Qiongzhou University as the experiment class. Firstly, the research team give the required students an entrance examination. Then, the experiment class take classes with 3D textbooks in multi-media classroom for 4 hours every week. Thirdly, the research team are also responsible for their final English examination. Both the scores in the two exams can be seen in the appendix. The data is analyzed by SPSS 16.0. The following is the research explanation.

Table 5.3.1   Check if there is no significant difference between the two exams

Research Hypothesis	There is no significant difference between the two exams.
Significance Level	.05
1- or 2-tailed	2-tailed
Research Design	
Dependent Variable	Scores
Measurement	Interval
Independent Variable	Students
Measurement	Nominal
Independent or Repeated-measured	Repeated
Statistical Procedure	T-test

By analyzing the data in the appendix with SPSS 16.0, our research team got Table 5.3.2 and Table 5.4 as follows. The result in Table 5.3.2 （t=-6.54, p=0.00<.01）tells us that there is significant difference between the two examinations.

Table 5.3.2   The result of whether there is significant difference between the pre-and post-exams

							T	Df	Sig. （2-tailed）
	\multicolumn{6}{c}{Paired Differences}			
		Mean	Std. Deviation	Std. Error Mean	\multicolumn{2}{c}{95% Confidence Interval of the Difference}			
					Lower	Upper			
Pair 1	Pre-post	-6.233 33	5.217 23	.95253	-8.181 48	-4.285 19	-6.544	29	.000

And the result of MEAN in Table 5.4 tells us that the scores of post examination are higher, which means that students learning 3D textbook for four hours every week could get better scores in English test.

Table 5.4 The result tells which exam's score has been imporved

Paired Samples Statistics

		Mean	N	Std. Deviation	Std. Error Mean
Pair 1	Pre	75.533 3	30	9.115 10	1.664 18
	Post	81.766 7	30	9.316 96	1.701 04

5.6.3 Optimized Technological Ecological Environment Improving Learning

The design of course modules should be built on both theoretical foundations which have absorbed all reasonable parts of various teaching theories（such as task-based learning of Constructivism, imitation and drills of Behaviorism, interactive activities of Communication Theory and so on.）and the practical foundations which fully grasp learners' study needs.

In short, the course design should take in the best aspects of each teaching theory. According to the actual learning requirement, it should felicitously deal with the triadic relationship among papery textbook, multimedia disks and network learning platform. The papery textbook, the main or basic element, emphasizes meaningful input, task-based exercises and instructive practices, being simple and comprehensive. The multi-media disk, the supplementary element, signifies its teaching content tri-dimensionally, enhancing learners' learning effect and arousing their interest. The network learning platform, the stretcher, is the extension and development of learning content, learning methods and learning evaluation. In other words, based on the teaching syllabus, the main content of the platform is closely connected with the main topic of textbooks to deepen and widen each topic. These three elements are not just inter-linked, interactive, but also inter-changed, inter-supplemented, forming an organic and integral teaching structure.

As for the formulation of 3D learning and teaching software, English teachers are responsible for the collection, arrangement and selection of various text, images, animation, videos and so on; and the education experts should design the content from the perspective of pedagogy and cognition, in order to ensure a reasonable arrangement of knowledge structure. The arrangement of knowledge should follow the cognition rules in a proper sequence. Meanwhile, the software development engineers are in charge of varied technological means, to optimize all the learning resources selected by English teachers. These engineers should help realize teachers' and experts' teaching assumptions. In the whole process of scheming, designing, exploiting and producing of teaching software, teachers, education experts and computer software developers should jointly participate in the teamwork and cooperate with each other. That could avoid over-development and over-production, reduce the deficiency and weakness of software, and prevent the imbalance between learners and course software. Thus, each element should be in proper position without unlimited performance.

After integration, the computer has been a common and regular tool in foreign language learning process, casting its influence on each student, each class and each learning link. Thus, it is not the teachers' exclusive and specialized presentation tool, but an organic part of foreign language course and learning. Through optimization, the computer plays many irreplaceable roles in the ecological environment for foreign language learners. Instead, it is an encouraging tool for students' learning, a communicative tool among students, an assisting tool for students' self-learning, a feedback tool for digital learning evaluation, an expressive tool for learning achievement and so on. The natural development of computers' super-power can effectively promote students' learning methods, and make new element blend into the whole system, to further stabilize the comprehensive function of the unbalanced environment.

In order to find out whether the role of computer has changed or not in learners' eyes, the research team surveyed 30 students from Qiongzhou University. Actually, the team set ten choices in term of the roles of computers in multi-media English class. From 1 to 10, they are respectively *a presentation tool for teaching content, a concrete showing tool for teaching principles, a tool for teachers' timely feedbacks and evaluations, a communicative tool for teachers and students, an assisting tool for individuals' learning, a heuristic tool for learning mode, a realization tool for learning objectives, an encouraging tool for arousing students' interest, a preparatory tool for students' preview* and *a checking tool for students' accomplishment*. Then the investigators ask the 30 students to rank the ten roles of computers from 1 to 5, according to their own situation. Rank 1 means that one thinks this role is totally unimportant. Rank 2 is basically unimportant. Rank 3 means occasionally important. Rank 4 is basically important. Rank 5 is quite important. From Graph 5.10, we can arrive at the following conclusions:

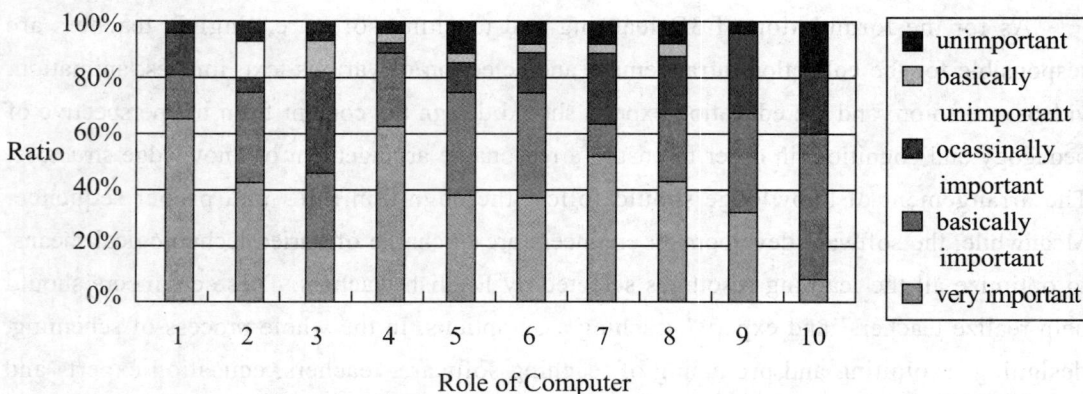

Graph 5.10　Position-setting Made by Students Towards the Role of Computer

67% of them regard that the role of computer functioning as *a presentation tool for teaching content* is quite important; 17% think it is basically important; 13% occasionally important; while 3% feel it is totally unimportant.

43% of them consider the role of computer as *a concrete showing tool for teaching principles* is quite important; 30% of them suppose it is basically important; 7% think it is occasionally important; while 13% of the students feel it is basically unimportant; 7% of them totally unimportant.

As for the role of being *a tool for teachers' timely feedbacks and evaluations*, 20% of them find it is quite important, 30% of them basically important; 33% of them occasionally important; while 10% think it is basically unimportant; and 7% of them totally unimportant.

With regard to the role of being *a communicative tool for teachers and students*, 63% of them think it is quite important; 27% of them basically important; 3% of them occasionally important; while 3% of them feel it is basically unimportant; and 3% of them totally unimportant.

37% of them see the role of *an assisting tool for individuals' learning* as quite important; the same percentage think it is basically important; 13% of them occasionally important; meanwhile, 3% regard it basically unimportant; 10% of them totally unimportant.

About the role of being *a heuristic tool for learning mode*, 37% of them agree that it is quite important; another 37% of them think it is basically important; 17% of them occasionally important; only 3% of them feel it is basically unimportant; and the rest 7% of them totally unimportant.

Half of the college students consider that computers are mainly functioning as *a realization tool for learning objectives*, which they think is quite important; 13% of them think this role is basically important; 27% of them occasionally important; while 27% of them think it is basically unimportant; 3% of them basically unimportant; and the rest 7% of them totally unimportant.

43% of them show their consent that the role of computers as *an encouraging tool for arousing students' interest* is quite important; 27% of them basically important; and 17% of them occasionally important. On the contrary, 7% of them think it is basically unimportant, whilt another 7% of them totally unimportant.

Mentioning the role of computers being *a preparatory tool for students' preview*, 33% of them find it quite important; 37% of them basically important; 27% of them occasionally important; but 3% of them feel it is totally unimportant.

As for the last role of computers being *a checking tool for students' accomplishment*, 10% of them suggest it is quite important; 50% of them basically important; 23% of them occasionally important; while 17% of them think it is totally unimportant.

5.6.4 Optimized Emotional Ecological Environment Improving Learning

Through optimization, learners should regard information technology as a cognitive tool for autonomous learning and an emotionally encouraging tool. Learners should take full advantage of their initiative and creation during the learning process, thus to make them the real subject of informational process and the object of knowledge infusion. In the context of independent exploitation, multi-level communication, cooperative learning and shared resources, learners should respect each other, communicate harmoniously, and cooperate interactively, to create an active and harmonious learning environment.

Secondly, teachers play a leading role in optimizing emotional learning ecological environment for students. They make students relaxed and pleasant by helping them to think actively. After clarifying the regularity of students' thinking, teachers can get down to helping students set a positive attitude towards network learning, which will enable them to realize that an earnest learning attitude can lead to learning responsibility and enthusiasm for participating in teaching activities and for overcoming difficulties. Such a kind of attitude will inevitably improve students' learning effect. Under the background of computer networks, teachers can't exert such subtle instructions face to face, but they can offer help with network courses, emails, discussion forums and other network communication ways. For example, in the introduction part of the course, teachers should remind students of an active network learning; it is of necessity to set up a check-up system for the teachers to stipulate them to regularly examine students' electronic learning records; it is a must to timely remind and care about students with passive learning or abnormal behavior by emails or other communication tools; it is helpful to guide the students to take part in learning with an active attitude by designing discussion topics in teaching discussion area.

Self-efficacy is an important motivation factor which influences students' self-learning. A good self-efficacy is based on successful operation, providing students with moderate difficult learning tasks. Students will experience the joy of success when they have finished tasks, thus their sense of self-efficacy will be strengthened. Teaching research shows that if the learning task is too difficult to be completed, this will push the students to the edge of helplessness, causing a sense of failure, and their learning motivation will be reduced; if the learning task is too easy, the students will think that accomplishing this simple task can't reflect their learning ability, let alone enhance their self-efficacy. Therefore, when the teacher is arranging the course assignments for the students, they should take students' individual differences and different knowledge accumulations into account. It is necessary to control the difficulty of learning tasks in order to make most of the students to let them complete it with efforts. Teachers can design some open questions, which generally intrigue students' thinking.

Students on different levels can look for materials and answer questions according to their ability, avoiding the great difficulty of task and contusion of enthusiasm. Optimization can further expand the monitoring function of network teaching platform, which allows teachers to monitor learners' operation progress at any time, and assess students learning situation timely. Teachers should help students think in depth, design appropriate learning activities and monitor the implementation of learning activities.

As for online teaching, learners' study effect is checked mainly through online testing and course exams. There are learners who can't achieve a desired result for various reasons in each exam. Without the encouragement and guidance of teachers, the students might attribute their failure to their inadequate ability or the great difficult academy, thus, these network learners are likely to have sense of negativity, anxiety, low self-esteem, even affecting their future study. Therefore, teachers should flexibly make use of attribution theory, by initiating votes, to trigger a collective discussion, and to lead students into a positive attribution. After students have the initial attribution by vote and response, teachers should check the voting results in time, classify the votes into sorts, and elect the most important types of attribution （ability, effort, task difficulty or other factors）. As for these selected factors, teachers should make timely assessment and feedback, pointing out whether learners attribution is appropriate or not, to correct attribution bias and make a more comprehensive analysis, and guide students to make a controlled, unstable factors （effort orientation） attribution. Generally speaking, the attribution on students' ability of making progress can make them gradually convinced that he has the learning ability; the attribution on students' effort of making progress can let them feel that they have the ability to control their step and thus will enhance their learning self-efficacy. As regard to those who doubt their learning capabilities, especial attribution on success should be done.

The integrated foreign language learning is featured by complex and diverse learning tasks. So students are easily frustrated, and often feel they have no capability or ways to accomplish them. It is necessary to first optimize students' ability of setting up learning plans and then to improve their emotional learning environment. First of all, let students set their own learning goals with clear positioning according to their actual situation. Students can also improve their learning effect by changing their goals into higher ones. Of course, students' learning objectives should be specific, clear, operational and easily detected.

Secondly, teachers should teach students how to make common objectives into individual goals. Usually, the objective of a network course is jointly developed by teachers. The curricula, lesson plans, and learning progress may not be suitable for all the learners. Teachers can encourage learners to transfer the common objective into an effective learning goal with unity and individuality, which is consistent with learners' personal features.

Thirdly, the network instructor can exploit the steps to help students develop a good habit of effectively using and managing time. The steps are to start a discussion, to spread the concept of time management, to set up plans, to implement the plans and to reflect on the discussion.

Finally, teachers should help students out of informational disorientation. The choice of presenting learning resources should be in line with adults' cognitive laws. A nice design should help learners to allocate their attention and time effectively. The content should be fair in structure, distinct in knowledge classification, and progressive in teaching content; the form should be simple and consistent; the layout of screen should agree with the characteristics of visual perception; the amount of information should be moderate enough to develop students' ability of filtering information and autonomously managing organizations.

It is often said that a real-time feedback of an error correction is very effective. However, would this feedback make students more nervous and let them make more mistakes? To answer this, three different computer tests are given, each test with two parts. When the students are doing the first test, teachers are asked to sit beside the 18 students. Whenever the students make a mistake, the teacher would immediately stop him and correct it. In the second test, teachers are also asked to sit beside the 18 students. If students make a mistake, the teacher nearby will help them correct it later. In the third test, we let students finish the test independently, and then tell them the wrong part. Each second part of the test will be finished by students independently. Each exercise will include 10 parts where they might make a mistake. The best grade is 0.10 points signify ten mistakes students make. These results will be used as the research data, seen in the appendix. The research team want to test whether there are significant differences among these three tests, and if it exists, where these differences are reflected. The research design is below:

Table 5.5.1 Check if there are significant differences among these three tests

Research Hypothesis	There are significant differences among these three tests.
Significance Level	.05
1- or 2-tailed	2-tailed
Design	
Dependent Variable	Error
Measurement	Scores Based on Ten Scales
Independent Variable	Assignment/Test
Measurement	Nominal
Independent or Repeated-measured	Repeated
Statistical Procedure	Friedman Test

Table 5.5.2　The result of the experiment of error correction

Test Statisticsa

N	18
Chi-Square	8.704
Df	2
Asymp. Sig.	.013

a. Friedman Test

The Friedman test shows that there are significant differences among the three tests at the 5 percent level （p=.013<.05） in Table 5.5.2. Then the investigators conduct a post hoc test to show where the difference lies. The analysis results in Table 5.6 show that the differences lie in test 2 and test 3.

Table 5.6　The result tells where the difference lies in the error correction experiment

Pairwise Comparisons

Measure: MEASURE_1

（I）Factor 1	（J）Factor 1	Mean Difference （I-J）	Std. Error	Sig.ᵃ	95% Confidence Interval for Differenceᵃ	
					Lower Bound	Upper Bound
1	2	-.611	.531	.797	-2.021	.799
	3	.944	.439	.138	-.221	2.110
2	1	.611	.531	.797	-.799	2.021
	3	1.556*	.437	.007	.395	2.716
3	1	-.944	.439	.138	-2.110	.221
	2	-1.556*	.437	.007	-2.716	-.395

Based on estimated marginal means

a. Adjustment for multiple comparisons: Bonferroni.

*. The mean difference is significant at the .05 level.

The conclusion is that teachers' timely reminder of students' mistake making will influence students' scores. In other words, teachers' teaching strategies will affect learners' learning effect. To some extent, the optimized emotional learning environment, in particular, the optimized teaching strategies of teachers, could significantly improve foreign language learners' learning.

◆ 5.7 ◆

Inspiration on Foreign Language Learning from Empirical Research

In order to get good understanding of the current situation of college students' autonomous learning under the optimized cyber-based environment, the research team designed a questionnaire on self-learning with 50 questions, and surveyed 30 students in Qiongzhou University. The questionnaire is clearly placed in the appendix. The following Graph 5.11 offers the results from the original data.

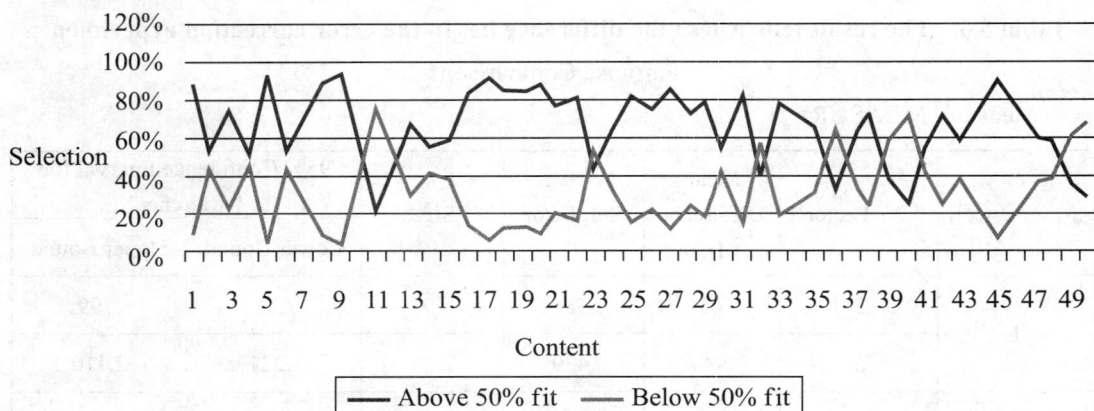

Graph 5.11　The Current Situation of College Students' Autonomic Learning Under the Cyber-based Environment

90% of them choose to live in school because the campus environment is good and cheap for study. 57% of them find the school library well-stocked and a quiet place for study; 77% of them say that they can always find their favorite books there, and 57% of them would borrow books or read in library at least once every week. 93% of college students think that the light of the classroom is right, and 57% of them say that they self-study in classrooms every day, and 70% of them think the self-study hour is over 2 hours every day. 90% of them tell us that there are Internet ports in their school dormitories, and 97% of them suppose they can always search the study resources needed on the Internet. 63% of them generally know the teaching hours required by college English courses, but only 27% of them know the multi-media teaching hours; 53% of them know how many hours English teacher spend to lecture an unit; 70% of them understand the specific course requirements for college English course; 57% of them generally know the teaching aims in each college English class; 60% of them know the assessment methods for the learning results in college English course; 87% of them think they know the exam types of college English course.

In the process of college English learning, 93% of students have set up learning goals, and 87% of them think they can achieve the goal; according to the learning goals, 87% of them have framed related learning plans; in the process of implementing their learning plans, 90% of them feel it is a little bit difficult, 80% of them say they need teachers' guidance and 83% of them need their classmates' help and encouragement.

Before schooling, 47% of them would go to bookstores to buy a teaching disk matched with college English textbooks; before class, 70% of them would preview the lessons by disks, videos or other audio-visual products; 77% of them would search for materials related to the topic on the Internet; and in the process of preparing a lesson, 83% of them would mark the questioning place. When having English class, 87% of them would listen to the teachers while browsing the PPT; 73% of them would join in English dialogue or mini-drama; 80% of them would have a discussion with teacher and classmates. After class, 57% of them usually copy teachers' teaching courseware; 83% of them like the pictures, sounds and flashes in teachers' courseware.

Only 40% of students find that their English teachers would communicate with them by network course or emails; 80% students say that their English teachers had given advices for English learning methods; 70% of them say that their English teachers would usually remind them to use English learning methods; 67% of them think these English learning methods are effective; only 37% of them will check and record their own learning dynamic condition with network course platform; 63% of students take exam scores to measure the effect of learning methods; 73% of them find that their college English teachers would regularly assign homework; 40% of them find that their college English teachers would regularly organize students' self-learning; only 27% of students think that their English teachers would give feedbacks on their dynamic learning conditions at any time.

When they are using network course platform for college English study, 57% of them would compete with other classmates; 73% of them would cooperate with others; 60% of them would participate in role-play; and 73% of them would have a group discussion with others.

Generally speaking, 93% of them are fully aware of the importance of media in foreign language learning; 77% of them think that they are good at using network tools and technology to store learning materials; 63% of them believe that they could integrate and reconstruct new knowledge with old knowledge; 40% of them would introduce the English learning in multi-media class to friends; 37% of them would communicate with family members about feelings of learning English in multi-media class; and only 30% of them would summarize the English learning results using multimedia networks.

Studies have shown that the students hold a positive attitude towards network English teaching and learning. At same time, the new models and methods have posed new challenges for teachers and students, requiring a joint effort made by teachers and students to maximize the advantage of network resources and to achieve an optimal learning effect. College English Curriculum Requirements clearly requires that the design of college English course should massively use advanced information technology and promote computer and cyber-based English teaching, to provide students with good language learning environment and conditions. Campus teaching and learning should be an important intermediary and carrier of teaching information. The application of modern information technology, especially with the support of network technology, makes English teaching out of the constraints of time and place towards the direction of individualization and autonomous learning. This requirement also tells us that the establishment of college English learning resource platform based on network technology and the autonomous online learning conforms to the college English teaching reform and its development trend. To have a better understanding of students' motivation, attitude, learning approaches and methods of network teaching and learning, as well as their feedbacks on learning effect, is helpful for network learning towards a healthy, effective and high-quality direction. The integration of foreign language courses needs students' more initiative and participation. A lot of activities and assignments require students' pro-active attitude. Meanwhile, their sufficient literacy of computer networks is required, such as knowledge about computer technology and network operation; regular monitoring and assessment towards self-learning, a controlled way of self-learning rather than an entirely free style, is also required.

The role of teachers has changed dramatically. In the situation of new teaching model, teachers' role has transferred from a transmitter of language knowledge and skills to a task designer, instructor, facilitator, organizer, manager and evaluator. Teachers should propose concrete teaching tasks according to the teaching requirements and textbook characteristics. Teachers need to invest more time and energy in effective designing, in order to achieve the teaching objectives. In the part of students' self-study or discussion, teachers should give positive guidance, continuous inspiration and encouragement, to make the communication and exchange continuous and deepen. At the same time, a teacher should be an outstanding manager to guide students into an active and positive learning at any time, so that the students would actively participate in various teaching links with mutual exchange and cooperation. Teachers should also be equipped with computer-network knowledge to meet their teaching needs. For example, as the network-based language laboratory is a huge learning resource pool, if students study here without their teachers' guidance and control, like the needles in the haystack, it is difficult for them to find the focus of learning and the knowledge they need. In particular, for some students with less self-control, it is easy for them to be in "informational disorientation" under the background of computer networks. Therefore, teachers must give necessary supervision to the open language laboratory and provide students with guidance about learning content and methods. For example, teachers can select websites for students in the process of cyber-based study, propose the learning scope, assign learning tasks to students, and establish a feedback bridge for online communication and conduct information exchange between teachers and students. The autonomous learning of foreign language is the future trend, but only under the guidance and supervision of teachers can independent study be the core content of self-learning.

In order to find out whether the role of teachers has changed or not in learners' eyes, the research team surveyed 30 students from Qiongzhou University. Actually, the team set eight roles for teachers in the context of multi-media English class. From 1 to 8, they respectively are *course designers, course developers, course lecturers, course organizers, course trainers, course evaluators, course assistants,* and *learning material providers.* Then the investigators ask the 30 students to mark each computer's role from Rank 1 to Rank 5, according to students' own situation. Rank 1 means that one thinks this role is totally unimportant. Rank 2 is basically unimportant. Rank 3 means occasionally important. Rank 4 is basically important. Rank 5 is quite important. From Graph 5.12, we can draw out the following conclusions:

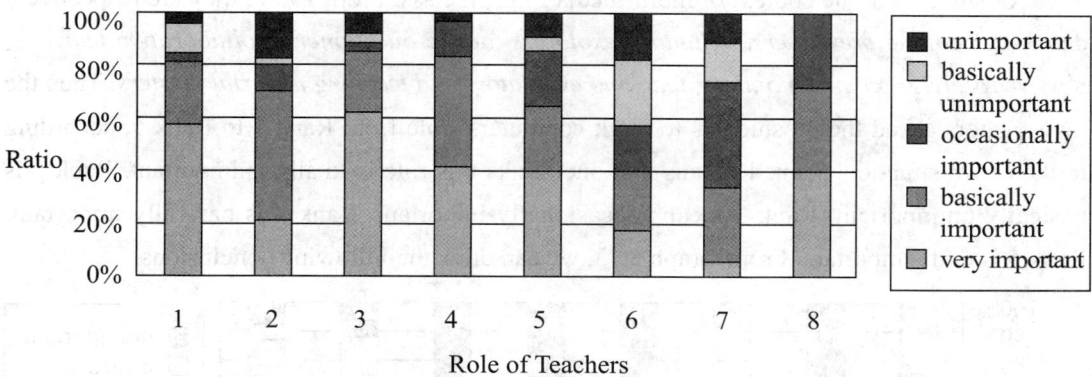

Graph 5.12   Position-setting Made by the Students Towards the Role of Teachers

57% of them think teachers' role as *course designers* is quite important; 27% of them feel basically important; 3% of them occasionally important; while 10% of them find it basically unimportant; 3% of them totally unimportant.

As for the role of *course developers*, 23% of them find it is quite important; 47% of them basically important; 10% of them occasionally important; while 3% of them think it is basically unimportant; and 17% of them totally unimportant.

63% of them consider teachers' role of *course lecturers* is quite important; 23% of them suppose it is basically important; 3% of them think it is occasionally important; while 3% of them feel it is basically unimportant; 7% of them totally unimportant.

With regard to the role of *course organizers*, 43% of them think it is quite important; another 43% of them basically important; 10% of them occasionally important; while 3% of them feel it is basically unimportant.

40% of them see the teachers' role of *course trainers* as quite important; 27% of them think it is basically important; 23% of them occasionally important; meanwhile, 3% of them regard it basically unimportant; 7% of them totally unimportant.

About the role of *course evaluators*, 17% of them say it is quite important; another 23% of them think it is basically important; 17% of them occasionally important; at the same time, 27% of them feel it is basically unimportant; 17% of them totally unimportant.

7% of them regard the role of *course assistants* to be quite important; 27% of them think it is basically important; 40% of them occasionally important; by contrast, 17% of them think it is basically unimportant; another 10% of them totally unimportant.

As for the last teachers' role as *learning material providers*, 40% of them suggest it is quite important; 30% of them basically important; and the rest 30% of them occasionally important.

In order to find out whether the role of students has changed or not in learners' eyes, the research team surveyed 30 students from Qiongzhou University. Actually, the team set eight roles for students in the context of multi-media English class. From 1 to 8, they are respectively defined as *course previewers, voluntary explorers, active questioners, collaborative learners, passive receivers, course monitors, teaching evaluators and learning material masters*. Then the investigators asked the 30 students to mark computers' role from Rank 1 to Rank 5, according to their own situation. Rank 1 means that one thinks this role is totally unimportant. Rank 2 is basically unimportant. Rank 3 means occasionally important. Rank 4 is basically important. Rank 5 is quite important. From Graph 5.13, we can draw the following conclusions:

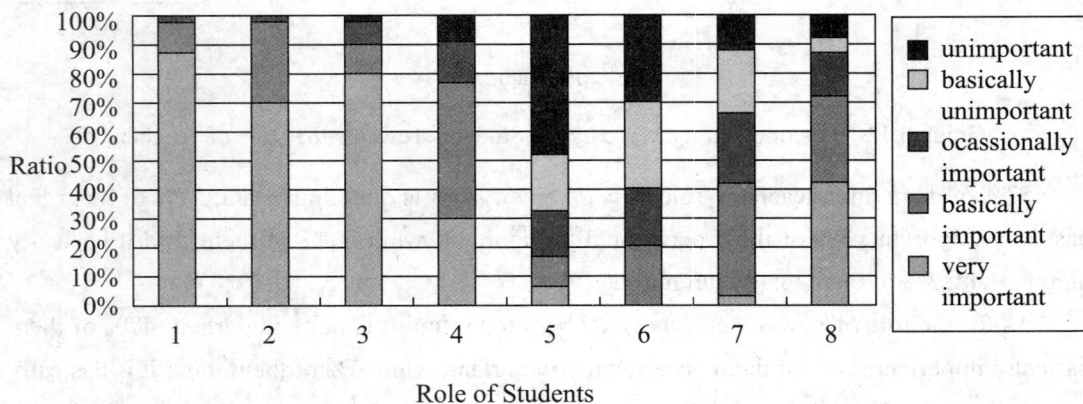

Graph 5.13 Position-setting Made by the Students Towards the Role of Learners

87% of them regard the role of student as *course previewers* quite important; 10% of them think it is basically important; and 3% of them occasionally important.

70% of the students consider the role of students as *voluntary explorers* quite important; 27% of them suppose it is basically important; and the rest 3% of them think it is occasionally important.

As for the role of being an *active questioners*, 80% of them find it quite important; 10% of them basically important; 7% of them occasionally important; while 3% of them totally unimportant.

With regard to the role of being *collaborative learners*, 30% of the students think it is quite important; 47% of them basically important; 17% of them occasionally important; while 7% of them totally unimportant.

Only 7% of the students see the student's role of *passive receivers* as quite important; 10% of them think it is basically important; 17% of them occasionally important. Meanwhile, 20% of them regard it basically unimportant; 47% of them totally unimportant.

About the role of being *course monitors*, 20% of them think it is basically important; another 20% of them consider it occasionally important. By contrast, 30% of them feel it is basically unimportant, and another 30% of them totally unimportant.

7% of the students consider that students are functioning as *teaching evaluators*, which is quite important, while 37% of them think it is basically important. 23% of them consider it occasionally important, basically unimportant, and the rest 13% of them totally unimportant.

Considering the last role of students being *learning material masters*, 43% of the students agree that it is quite important; 30% of them basically important; 13% of them occasionally important; while 7% of them think it is basically unimportant and another 7% of them totally unimportant.

With the integration of computer networks into foreign language curriculum, students' learning environment falls into imbalances. Primarily, the structure of learning system had undergone fundamental changes. The traditional teaching-oriented learning structure had changed into both a student-main body and teacher-leading learning structure. Through the empirical research in Chapter 5, it is found that at this stage some colleges and universities have already achieved this student-centered learning mode which lays equal stress on teaching and learning. Teachers play the roles of practitioners, designers, facilitators and managers in the study process, while students become the practitioners, designers and executers. Through investigation, it is also reflected that under the background of computer networks, students have high expectations for their teachers' help in foreign language learning. Therefore, student-centered self-learning is not ideal. After optimizing learning environment, students, teachers, computer technology, learning content and other elements are developing harmoniously.

The environment is of great help to students' self-learning as well as teachers' supervision by answering students' questions and assessing their learning results. In addition, learning resources, equipment building, emotional psychology and other co-factors coordinate with each other, creating a harmonious, dynamic and developed learning environment. In order to maintain the ecological nature of the learning environment, teachers should provide students with various learning content and activities to give them more options. Therefore, the key to the establishment of an ecological environment is to design diversified learning resources and activities to better meet students' various needs.

Constructing the Model of Foreign Language Learners' Cyber-based Learning Environment

As mentioned above, the construction and optimization of cyber-based ecological learning environment for foreign language learners are completed mainly from two aspects: one is from the perspective of ecological niche by defining micro environmental factors （individual, group and group chain） and macro-environment factors （foreign language education policy, learning mode, students' self-regulation, information and learning resources, available facilities for learning, informationalized learning）. From this perspective, to construct the ecological environment by finding out reasonable niches of the elements within the ecological environment to optimize their overall function becomes the aim; while from the ecological perspective, the four sub-environments are re-examined, which aims to optimize the internal structure of each sub-environment to enhance learners' learning adaptability. Through these two levels of optimization, the ultimate goal is to establish a harmonious, dynamic and positive cyber-based ecological learning environment for foreign language learners and improve learning efficiency and learning effect. In this respect, the author attempts to build a mode of cyber-based ecological learning environment for foreign language learners from an ecological perspective. First and foremost, we should have a general idea of the characteristics of this environment, three interactive relationships and three ecological relationships within this ecological environment.

6.1

Characteristics of Cyber–based Learning Ecological Environment

6.1.1 Systematic Integrity

After optimization, the cyber-based ecological learning environment for foreign language learners emphasizes its systematic integrity which refers to the interrelationships and interactions among various elements of the ecosystem, as well as the unity of their functions. In other words, the cyber-based ecological learning environment is a functional entity characterized by mutual interactions between learners and various ecological factors.

It is the combination of the constituent elements, thus of systematic integrity. In the cyber-based ecological learning environment with good systematic integrity, the ecological factors are interdependent and mutually conditioned which can lead to the unity of their functions and effects, thus achieving the optimization of the overall functionality of the system. For example, in the cyber-based ecological learning environment, the arrangement of learning resources should be consistent with the design of learning activities; the choice of learning strategies should be compatible with the design of learning content or activities. In this way, there will be smoothness and consistency in the process of students' learning, thus to the maximum degree resulting in quick absorption of knowledge and the construction of implications based on understandings.

In the four sub-environments, because individuals have different cognitive levels, emotional experiences, etc., and all environmental factors also have different attributes and functions, one can not be substituted by another. Nonetheless, all elements are interlinked and interactive in this learning environment, constituting an organic entirety.

6.1.2 Stable Balance

After optimization, the cyber-based ecological learning environment for foreign language learners attaches great importance to dynamic balance. This indicates that within a certain period of time there is high-level adaptation and coordinated unity between learners and cyber-based learning environment, as well as among the various ecological factors.

At this time, the internal structures and external functions are relatively stable in the ecological learning environment. A good ecological environment for computer-based learning should have good balance, which can make the learning environment maximize its resources. Moreover, the ecological balance within the foreign language learners' cyber-based environment is a dynamic balance. Or rather, the influence of any internal and external factor is likely to break this balance, causing an ecological imbalance of the network-based learning environment and cause thorough disorder of the entire system. For example, in this learning eco-environment, the ratio between learners and facilitators, or technical supporters, or teaching administrators, should be kept within a certain degree, achieving different levels of balance between learners' needs for guidance, teachers' capability of instruction, supportive efficiency from technical staff, and administrators' planning and management. Because of this, the learning effect and use of human resources will be optimized. If this kind of balance is broken, an ecological imbalance of the network learning environment will occur, resulting in decreasing of learning effect or waste of huma n resources.

The computer-network-based learning environment has its own specific structure and function, composed of a variety of ecological factors such as teachers, students, teaching materials, curriculum, equipment, networks, technical staff, teaching management personnel. In this environment, all elements are constantly involved in the material flow, information flow, energy flow and emotional flow with interactions and mutual influences.

6.1.3 Dynamic Openness

The optimized computer-network-based ecological environment for foreign language learners pays more attention to its openness, which is also a sub-environment of foreign language educational eco-environment. Meanwhile, it has specific characteristics of extreme openness of the network-based virtual world. Therefore, it is not a closed system but open to communicate and interact with the outside world in terms of material, energy information and emotion. There are three aspects for the openness: one is the openness of resources through information flow to achieve the updating of foreign language learners' existing knowledge.

Physical learning environment provides the material basis for learners and teachers. As a source of information, resourceful learning environment can provide information for learners and teachers. Technological learning environment, as its name shows, will on one hand facilitate learners' learning and on the other hand offer teachers teaching supports. In emotional learning environment, it is very important for learners to have good controlling and regulating abilities with good interactions, which is as important as the completion of learning tasks in that both are helpful in creating a better psychological and emotional environment. The whole progress of emotional exchanges is not static but dynamic. The second point of the openness refers to the fact that the four sub-environments enable learners to obtain more space and resources.

The key point to ensure the fresh vitality is to enhance the openness of the computer-network-based learning environment. For example, the resource design should be smart and diverse, including not only the existing resources within the environment but also inbound links to ensure the openness of resources. In the process of students' autonomy learning, learners should get assistance both from internal staff and from external experts, to ensure more information exchanges.

Sharing is the other characteristic of the openness of cyber-based ecological learning environment. Learners can take full advantage of computers and networks to obtain information and enrich learning content and learning methods. They can conduct all kinds of network learning activities, such as downloading software, conducting online communication to improve the learning effect, participating in the online electronic forum for foreign language learning, browsing news, attending foreign language contests online and so on. All these sharing experiences will guide the learners into a virtual foreign language learning class, enable them to enjoy a variety of extracurricular activities through network space and make them improve comprehensive abilities in using foreign language naturally and freely.

◆ 6.2 ◆
Three Interactive Relationships

The optimized foreign language learners' ecological environment attaches great importance to the influence of nature, society and humanism on learners' foreign language learning, as well as the interaction between learners and the environment. There exist a variety of factors in a harmonious foreign language learners' ecological environment in which the interdependence, mutual restraints, cooperation, competition, integration and coexistence of these ecological factors have maintained great vitality of learning environment.

The modern education teaching theory which regards "learning theory" as the core indicates that "learning" is a kind of activity that the cultural knowledge of society or group thoughts, concepts and ways of solutions to problems are absorbed and internalized by learners. Therefore, there are two aspects of learning content: one is "social cultural knowledge", which means the knowledge or curriculum system which is already spreading in the society and acknowledged by the public; the other is "the group thoughts, concepts and ways of solving problems", which refers to the thoughts, concepts and ways of solutions to problems, which are already shared by learners or to be formed during the learning process. Through the definition of learning, we can tell that learning is the interactions between learners and their learning environment or between learners and other learners for the gradual acquisition of knowledge. In foreign language learning environment based on computers and networks, we can see three important interactive relationships: teacher-learner, learner-learner and learner-computer.

6.2.1 Teacher-learner Relationship

As for the interaction between learners and teachers, it can be discussed from three aspects, namely, before-class learning, in-class learning and after-class learning. From this point of view, the balance of learning ecological environment will be broken once the teacher being an ecological factor is not compatible with learners or there is inconformity between teachers' teaching and learners' learning.

First of all, during the process of before-class learning, teachers are the designer and developer of learning curriculum. Due to the introduction of information technology into foreign language learning, students' curriculum are no longer the media for specific knowledge system, but the process of development that students and teachers both participate in to explore and gain knowledge, hence the teachers' role of developers and designers for foreign language curriculum.

Secondly, during the process of students' in-class learning, teachers can play the role of an organizer, trainer and evaluator in class. The teaching is based on students' existing knowledge and experience to train students' learning ability. Under the background of cyber-based teaching, learning activities in class and supervising interactions between students and learning software are equally important. Only in that way can we guarantee the efficiency and sustainability during the whole learning process. The students' training from teachers is conducted to help learners study effectively by making good use of learning strategies. For the evaluation on students' learning effect, teachers should take learners' final learning result into account. Consideration should also be given to students' learning attitudes, learning result in stages, improvement made in the learning process, etc.

Finally, in the process of after-class learning, the relationship between teachers and students are still interdependent and cooperative. Teachers should help students to conduct learning activities independently, make students adapt themselves to new ways of learning as soon as possible, and help them obtain and analyze all kinds of information effectively. As an intermediary agent between students and the information world, teachers should also provide Internet navigations to guide students to acquire and take advantage of reasonable information resources effectively to avoid the "information disorientation" phenomenon. Therefore, the assistant relationship between learners and teachers focuses on the point that teachers should provide and introduce learning methods to students, answer students' questions with enlightening implications and get students' feedbacks timely so as to truly improve their self-learning ability.

6.2.2 Learner-learner Relationship

Learner-learner relationship mainly includes two levels of interactions: interactions between learners and other learners; interactions between learners and learning facilitators. First of all, it is the interaction among learners, who can share collective wisdom and experience through direct or indirect interaction, and real time or non-real time interaction between learners and their learning partners in an environment of consultation and instruction, or an environment of mutual collaboration, or an environment of encouragement and evaluation, or an environment of digestion and innovation, or an environment of psychology and emotion, or an environment of science and technology with humanistic environment.

Secondly is the interaction between learners and facilitators, which is helpful to the further understandings of their partners' progress of learning and the existing or possible difficulties cropping up during the learning process, thus expecting timely and effective guidance or explanations from others. It is because all the members of the community share their opinions, viewpoints and emotions freely and open that the community can make continuous improvement and keep dynamic vitality. The continuous interaction among its members in the community is the vivid reflection of the coexistence of the community.

Based on the computer-based and network-based learning, it is possible to make learners interact with each other. The mode can be divided into the following five types:

First of all, competitive interaction. It means that two or more learners face the same learning content or context to learn and compete for the efficiency of achieving the objectives and requirements. Because of this competitive relationship, all learners can totally be involved in the learning which makes the learning effect relatively obvious. The disadvantage of this mode is that because individuals have different original levels of language competence, it tends to be hard to control the targeting learning content.

The second one is synergetic interaction, which means many learners assume a certain learning task together. During the learning process, every learner can choose whatever method he deems the most suitable and effective to cooperate with others while helping each other and relying on each other. During the cooperative process, learners can gradually get the right understanding and comprehension of learning content to finish the learning task with collective wisdom. The disadvantage of this mode is that it is sometimes difficult to deal with mutual coordination.

The third one is role-playing interaction which features that learners can play different roles of finishing learning tasks either in the form of teacher-learner role play or in the form of situational role play. The teacher-learner role play is to let learners play the roles of learners and guiders respectively, with one answering questions while the other checking, explaining and evaluating feedbacks. The situational role play requires that several learners play different roles separately according to the related learning subject in order to create a lifelike situation for foreign language learning. This form makes learners have a real feeling to understand the learning content and topic-related requirements. But the disadvantage for this mode is that it is hard to balance the learners' "knowledge difference" towards the learning task.

The fourth one is group evaluation interaction. This mode means that learners use their own practical experiences to evaluate the learning result by themselves, and through evaluation to prepare for their learning in the second stage. The purpose is to teach learners how to evaluate, giving reasonable evaluations not only to the learning efficiency of group members but also to the performance of the whole learning group in terms of its organization, schedule, progress, coordination and implementation. In this situation, the evaluation not only includes learners' learning condition, but also covers social and cultural aspects.

The fifth one is problem-solution interaction which belongs to task-target learning. To be specific, learners study with the method of solving some kind of problem. The key point is question setting which needs to be varied, not only meeting student's needs but also coordinated with the discipline of foreign language teaching and learning. When it comes to problem analysis, planning and classification of tasks are needed. As for the problem solving, learners should cooperate with each other to finish the learning task together.

In short, all kinds of modes have their pros and cons. In actual situations, flexibility is emphasized. For example, learners can use one or two modes when necessary. The foreign language learning under the new environment should enbale learners to have more cooperative learning opportunities and to finish group learning tasks through cooperative exchanges. The communication, interaction and different opinion exchanges can encourage each other to make a healthy competition and help learners gain more deep understandings of knowledge and ability cultivation. During the process of communication, learners' ways of thinking and the method of solving questions tend to be more distinct, favorable to forming a deeper level of thinking.

6.2.3 Learner-computer Relationship

The combination of multimedia foreign language teaching with network technology makes learners' learning individualized. Dealing well with the relationship between learners and computers can release the stress of self-learning and enhance their learning efficiency.

The appearance of language labs, the result of modern information technology, firstly provides individuals with a learning platform, with which students set their own learning steps in the process of learning, so-called "self-pacing". Timely feedbacks are available when learners are practicing. That is to say, students can clearly know their learning conditions, which is conducive to the improvement of their learning methods. Learners' initiatives and cooperation can be brought into full play if the relationship between learners and computers are well handled.

In this regard, we can know that the optimization of the cyber-based ecological environment for foreign language learners makes learners' learning virtual, personalized, broadened, co-operative and naturalized.

Through the investigation made by the author in local schools, currently the urgent ecological factors we need to optimize under the background of computers and networks are the integration of students' and teachers' recognition, learning content and software, as well as the enhancement of students' and teachers' network qualities and the guarantee of computer devices.

First of all, the anxiety of learners and teachers from networks and computers should be eliminated. Based on the familiaritiy with computers, learners and teachers should realize that computers and networks are an integral part of foreign language learning rather than one theory only. They should also be aware that the balanced cyber-based foreign language learning environment is the result of mutual functions of a number of interrelated factors and elements.

Secondly, the network learning resources are unlimited. When it comes to the integration of network content into related software, full considerations should be taken on learners' actual needs and teachers should enrich cyber-based learning activities according to the actual needs in class to promote the completion of learning objectives.

Besides, by strengthening trainings on information technology, skills and teaching methods, both teachers' and learners' network qualities should be accordingly enhanced. Finally, the most basic element is the guarantee of services which can be done from such aspects as the arrangement for the location of computer rooms, setup of computer classes, layout of computer classrooms, setup of preparation time for class, etc. For example, the layout of a classroom should be designed to facilitate the conduction of both cyber-based learning activities and daily teaching activities.

In addition, the poor interaction between learners and computers in terms of courseware designing lies in the following two aspects. One is that during the process of courseware making, designers do not take into account the unity and simplicity of the operation screen, and the random placement of buttons severely affect smooth interactions, which causes much inconvenience not only to the users but even to the designer himself. The other aspect is featured by poor flexibility and interactivity. The designed courseware has only a few jumping links and few exit links, which makes the users have no choice but to watch it from the beginning to the end and can't skip the meaningless part. Of course, they can't quit in halfway, resulting in great inconvenience.

To improve the human-computer interaction of the courseware, we must make full use of various input and output functions possessed by all kinds of multimedia tools. By designing questions, recording feedbacks and providing appropriate practices, we can stimulate students' learning initiatives and enthusiasm and make them totally involved in the learning process. In the production process, the courseware can be divided into different levels and different knowledge units according to the inner relations of the material, and then the tools can be used to make these units form a system with hypertext structure, thus providing convenience for students' skipping from one part to another. It will also allow students to choose the interesting part and temporarily suspend some of them to read the auxiliary content, and then return to the original part. In this way, each student takes what he needs, achieving what the traditional courseware can not.

Through the analysis of these three interactions, we make an attempt to construct a new learning model based on an integration of computers and networks into foreign language curriculum, as is shown in Figure 6.1.

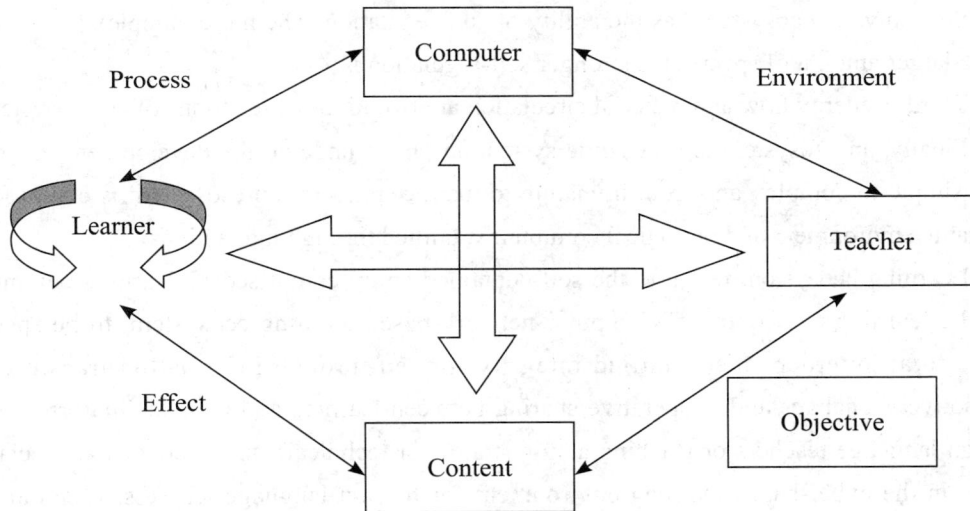

Figure 6.1   Cyber-based Ecological Learning Model

The figure shows that by optimizing the learning eco-environment, the relationships between learners, teachers, computers, and learning content are no longer one-way, but a kind of two-way interaction with interdependence and mutual conversion. Students have become active constructors of knowledge.

6.3

Three Ecological Relationships

6.3.1 Cyber-based Foreign Language Learners' Environment is an Ecosystem

The British ecologist A.G. Tansley （1935） first pointed out that "The so-called ecosystem includes the entire biological community and its physical and chemical factors, which constitute an integrated part of a natural system. However, in mature ecosystems, all these factors are almost in balance. The entire system is functioning through the interactions of these factors." Nowadays, people's interpretation of an ecosystem tends to be that an ecosystem is an unified integrity achieved by the interactions through energy flow and physical circulation between a variety of biological organisms and inorganic environment in a certain space and time. An ecosystem, natural or artificial, is of the following common features:

Firstly, an ecosystem is a major structural and functional unit in ecology theory, belonging to the highest research level of ecological theory.

Secondly, an ecosystem has the ability of self-regulation. The more complex the structure is, the larger amount of species the stronger self-regulation is.

Thirdly, energy flow and material circulation are two kinds of functions of an ecosystem.

Finally, an ecosystem is a dynamic system and must undergo the development process—from simple to complex and from immature to mature. In short, an ecosystem is composed of inorganic environment and biological community, unified through interactions.

Learning ecosystem refers to the self-contained entity comprised by learning community and the learning environment. Computer-network-based learning ecosystem, to be specific, refers to an interdependent unified integrity formed through information transmission, interactive exchanges and cooperative sharing between learners and their facilitators （either foreign language teachers or teaching administrators or technical staff or education specialists, etc.） in the cyber-based learning environment for foreign language learners. It can also be recognized as one sub-system of educational ecosystem.

Arthur Richardson pointed out that a learning environment is a kind of learning ecosystem consisting of learning resources and learning activities, so the diversity of resources and activities is the basic feature of learning environment ecosystem. The openness of biological ecosystem determines the openness of cyber-based learning ecological environment. In this environment, first of all, information is active in its input and output and learners' learning resources are very rich which laid a foundation for the formation of computer-based learning ecosystem, for the creation of students' effective learning and for the acquisition of the needed knowledge. Secondly, the main body of the environment is open too which means that they can voluntarily exchange or communicate with other learning subjects or external environment and similarly members outside are also allowed to be involved in this environment. All above show that the cyber-based learning environment for foreign language learners is not a closed system, but an ecologically open system constantly keeping with the outside to exchange information, conduct various learning activities and interact with other learners.

To sum up, by making comparisons between the cyber-based ecological learning environment to be optimized and the one already optimized, it is quite obvious that the optimized learning environment is generally stepping towards balanced development. Secondly, the optimized learning environment is an ecological system with balanced input and output of material flow, information flow, energy flow and emotional flow.

To the author, the optimized and balanced learning environment under the background of computer networks can be interpreted from three levels: macro-ecology, meso-ecology and micro-ecology. The ecological balance of macro-ecology displays the balance between the four sub-environments that is physical learning environment, resourceful learning environment, technological learning environment and emotional learning environment under the background of computers and networks. The ecological balance of meso-ecology is viewed from the balance between various ecological look at the ecological balance and it is a learning environment to achieve a balance between the various elements with the learning ecological environment. And the ecological balance of micro-ecology refers to the balance between internal factors in each sub-environment. The cyber-based ecological environment for foreign language learners itself is a big integrated system which covers all sides and aspects of each sub-environment. Moreover, each sub-environment forms a new ecosystem respectively. Within each independent sub-environment and system, various factors interact with each other through mutual adaptation, finally promoting the dynamic balance of the entire system in turn.

6.3.2 Cyber-based Foreign Language Learners' Environment Has Its Own Ecological Niche

Under the environment of computers and networks, the ecological learning environment for foreign language learners includes physical learning environment, resourceful learning environment, technological learning environment and emotional learning environment. Physical learning environment has such physical ecological factors as location, sunshine, lighting, such school factors as equipment management, device maintenance, such family factors as house network, family atmosphere, and factors in terms of policies and systems. Resourceful learning environment covers such ecological factors as learning materials, students' motivation, network qualifications and qualities for both teachers and students, network resources and so forth. Technological learning environment involves curriculum modules, technology software modules, etc. And emotional learning environment consists of psychological factors, interpersonal interactions and social acceptance or recognition.

Through optimization, each of these factors in the environment has its best time or space positioning suited for their survival. That is to say, all ecological factors are in the appropriate and dynamic niches. The result of examining and optimizing cyber-based learning ecological environment from ecological perspective is that whether it is an individual niche like a student, teacher, teaching administrator and technical staff or it is group niche like group of students and group of teachers, all ecological factors are playing their respective roles in their respective niches. For example, a teacher's dynamic niche can be interpreted as follows. Before class, a foreign language teacher acts as curriculum designers and developers, because the use of multimedia information technology makes curriculum no longer the specific carrier of knowledge, but a developing process that the teachers and students are both involved in the acquisition of knowledge. In class, the teachers play the role of organizers, trainers and evaluators, as under the multimedia and network teaching environment. Teachers should from time to time monitor the interaction between students and learning software or certain studying procedures in addition to the organization of students' various learning activities and promotion of foreign language teaching, with a purpose of ensuring the best condition of the entire learning process. After class, teachers are facilitators and providers of learning resources, which means that teachers should offer students certain assistance and guidance in the process of their autonomous learning so that students can adapt themselves to this new way of learning as soon as possible. Besides, in order to reduce the "disorientation" phenomenon, it makes sense for teachers to provide students with Internet navigation to effectively guide the students to have easy access to online materials and reasonably make use of rich information resources（Chen Jianlin 2010: 140）.

The cyber-based ecological environment for foreign language learners itself is an integrated and complete system which contains all aspects of foreign language curriculum, such as teachers, administrators, classrooms, course syllabus, learning methods, learning content, learning environment, learning efficiency assessment, information resources, information technology and so on, which can possibly be shown in the figure below.

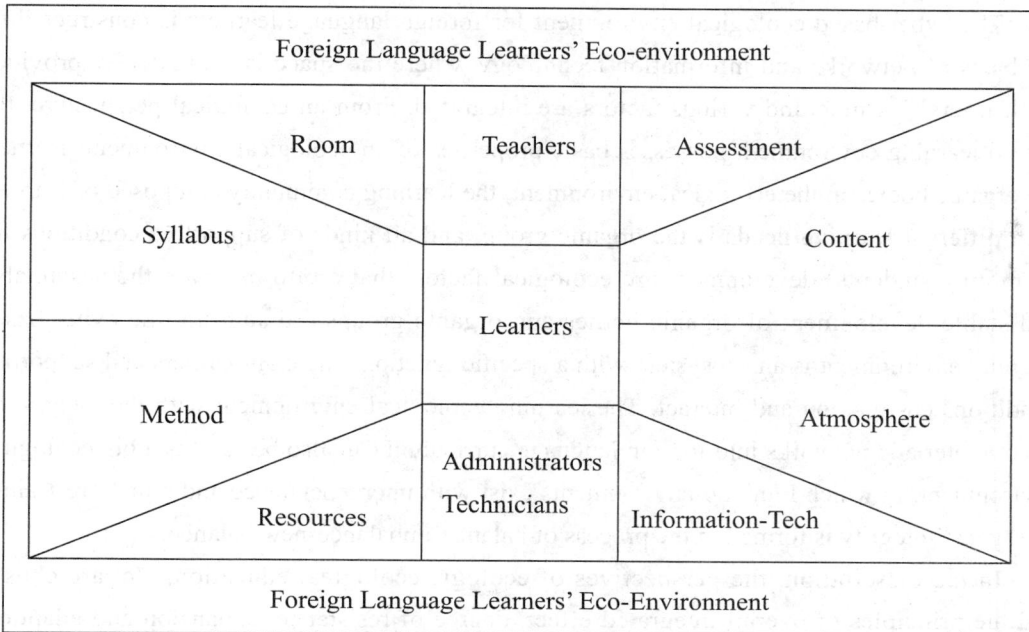

Figure 6.2   Cyber-based Ecological Learning Environment for Foreign
Language Learners Has Its Ecological Niche

6.3.3 Cyber-based Foreign Language Learners' Environment is an Ecological Environment

Ecological environment refers to an environment comprised by combined ecological factors, where individual, population or a community can have an impact on certain organisms (including humans). In educational environment, human beings are the main body and objects of educational activities. We can say that the human progress and social development are closely related to development of education. The development of education is inseparable from the ecological environment of education, which can be described as a kind of synergy and evolutionary relationship. The so-called ecological environment of education is a polynary ecosystem with multi-dimensional space, which have conditioned and regulatory influence on the generation, existence and development of education (Wu Dingfu & Zhu Wenwei 1990).

The latest theory on learning holds that the network needs to be generated in certain circumstances or environment, while the best definition of so-called "environment" is ecosystem, hence the generation of ecological network (Hu Zhuanglin 2008). Learning environment "is the integration of various supportive conditions aiming to promote learners' development" (Zhong Zhixian 2005: 35-41).

The cyber-based ecological environment for foreign language learners is constructed on the basis of networks and information technology, where the space is supportively provided for learners' learning and various factors are integrated. From an ecological perspective, the virtual learning environment possesses basic properties of an ecological environment: learners are organic bodies in the ecological environment; the learning community composed of learners with different learning needs is the organic group; and all kinds of supportive conditions for promoting students' development are ecological factors that are to maintain the sustainable and stable development of organic bodies and organic groups. To sum up, the cyber-based learning environment is an ecosystem with a specific function where all learners and supportive conditions co-function and interact. The learning ecological environment with the integration of computer and networks into foreign language curriculum can also be seen as a big ecological environment, in which four sub-environments exist with interdependence and mutual restraints. Its organic integrity is formed in the process of balance-imbalance-new balance.

In the dissertation, the perspectives of ecology, ecological education, etc. are chosen and the principles of overall integrated effect, degree of resistance, expansion and adaption, growth and restraint, etc. are used as breakthrough points to optimize the imbalanced ecological learning environment for foreign language learners resulting from the integration of computers and networks into foreign language curriculum, thus creating a dynamic, harmonious and systematic ecological foreign language learning environment.

Sustainable development seeks for a best ecosystem to maintain the ecological integrity and facilitate the achievement of human desires, thus keeping human environment sustainable. The ecological perspective to view cyber-based learning environment indicates that the cyber-based learning environment has provided convenient conditions for students' learning. The cyber-based learning environment should also follow the principles of sustainable development because only by constantly optimizing the imbalanced learning environment and timely updating its internal resources can we enhance the viability of the learning community and achieve the balance and sustainability of the entire cyber-based ecosystem.

After optimization, the cyber-based foreign language learning environment is not only an organic environment comprised by many interrelated and interacting parts or elements with a certain composition structure and a specific function, but also an ecological environment in which all ecological elements（learning objectives, learning content, learning methods, learning styles, learning time, learning materials, regulatory mechanisms, learning channels, etc.）are in mutual interactions and interdependence with balanced development.

6.4

Foreign Language Learners' Cyber-based Learning Environment Model

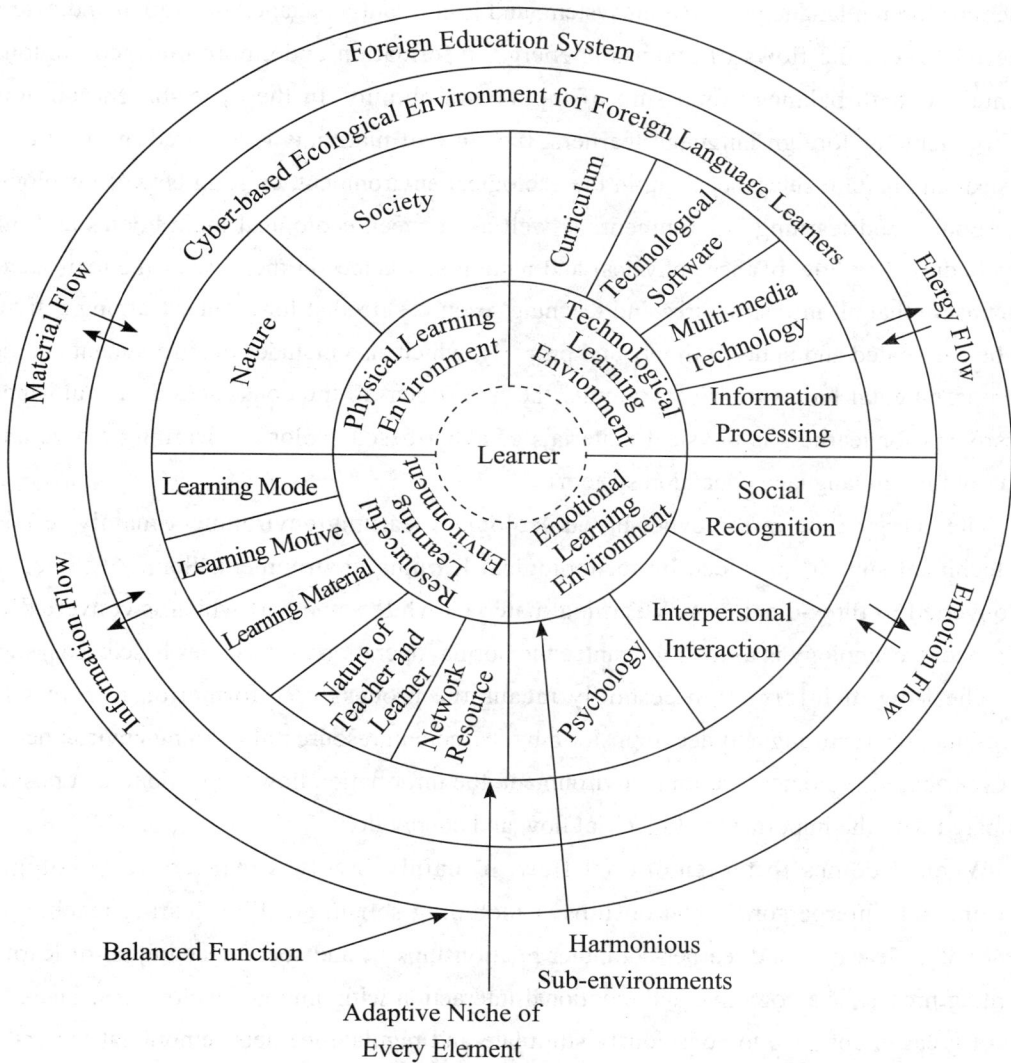

Figure 6.3   The Model of Cyber-based Ecological Environment for Foreign Language Learners

By conducting an analysis of optimizing the four sub-environments of cyber-based ecological environment for foreign language learners and the three interactive relationships within the environment, the author intends to construct a model of cyber-based ecological environment for foreign language learners from ecological point of view, as shown in Figure 6.3.

The figure above clearly shows the components of the cyber-based ecological environment for foreign language learners and its function in foreign language learners' learning process. The cyber-based ecological environment for foreign language learners is a sub-environment and sub-system of foreign language education system, and is constantly engaged in internal and external material, where the flows of materials, energy, information and emotion are continuously maintained with balanced total sum of inputs and outputs. In the cyber-based ecological environment for foreign language learners, the flow of materials is featured by the flow of physical and natural substances within the ecological environment, existing between ecological main bodies and learning environment, as well as between ecological main bodies and other main bodies. The flow of these physical and natural substances in the flow of the main factors is to ensure that all infrastructures and teaching resources needed for regular learning activities can be eliminated and updated timely and properly, which also includes the investment and flow of environmental hardware. For example, the investment in the construction of multi-media classrooms for learners is physical materials of cyber-based ecological learning environment input by foreign language education system.

The energy flow in the cyber-based ecological learning environment mainly refers to the technical support provided by technological learning environment. Some of the energy is converted to three-dimensional learning materials while some part which is converted into multimedia technology is used to guarantee the normal operation of the cyber-based ecosystem.

The flow of information certainly means the process of information transmission, processing, restructuring and decomposition by learners in resourceful learning environment. In the cyber-based ecological learning environment, the information flow is in a dominant position, compared with the importance of material flow and energy flow.

When it comes to the emotional flow, it mainly involves learners' psychological environment, interpersonal relationships（including self-interaction, learner-teacher, and learner-other learners, and learner-computer relationships）, and social recognition of learners. Learning process is a cognitive and emotional interaction with unified development. Therefore, it is of great importance to consciously stimulate and regulate learners' emotional factors and of great help to the balance and smoothness of emotional flow, as well as to the improvement of foreign language learning effect and enhancement of learners' personal development.

The shortage of energy flow and material flow will undoubtedly have a negative effect on the quality of constructing foreign language learning environment. Lack of information flow will affect learners' updating of learning concept and renewal of learning content and learning styles. The smoothness of emotion flow is the internal factor which will have a huge impact on learners' learning efficiency.

Sometimes, although there is big information flow and material flow within systems and environments, learners' learning quality will still be negatively influenced and the balance of learning ecological environment will still be broken if all flows move towards an incorrect direction. Similarly, if energy flow is inadequate in its supply or emotional flow is not well regulated or aroused, an imbalance of the entire learning environment will also be caused.

To sum up, according to the diagram above, the four sub-environments of physical learning environment, resourceful learning environment, technological learning environment and emotional learning environment are interdependent and mutually based. The balance of the entire cyber-based ecological learning environment depends on the balance of these four sub-environments and the fulfillment of function of subsystems. On the basis of these four sub-environments, various elements of the cyber-based learning environment are in interactive adaptations, and ultimately each element has found its proper and specific niche that is in good space-time position, maintaining the coherence and integrity of the overall function within the environment.

The core mechanism of ensuring the good functioning of foreign language learners' cyber-based ecological environment is to establish learner-centered learning mechanism. Through this mechanism, learners can carry out a variety of self-learning forms such as supportive learning, service-based learning, instructive learning, stimulating learning, luminous learning, and evaluation-based learning within the cyber-based learning ecological environment, truly transforming the computers' status from "auxiliary" to "normalized". The cyber-based ecological environment for foreign language learners, through the circulating operation of monitoring, regulation, improvement and optimization, will finally achieve foreign language learners' dynamic, healthy and sustainable development.

To conclude, the cyber-based ecological environment for foreign language learners, through optimization, is an integrated ecological environment which can reflect ecological laws and principles, can be adjusted, improved, optimized and developed, and can have a positive impact on foreign language learners' learning with learners being the center.

6.5
Results and Discussion

With the rapid development of information technology and continuous expansion of cyberspace, cyber-based foreign language learning has become an important style of learning and the construction of computer-based learning environment has also become an important area of research. The development of ecological research provides a new perspective for studying cyber-based ecological learning environment for foreign language learners, which can help us construct a balanced ecological learning environment.

From ecological point of view, there are a series of practical problems existing in the current foreign language learning environment which can be regarded as the detailed phenomenon of ecological imbalance. Through the optimization of the imbalanced learning environment, these problems can be avoided. The basic principles and laws of ecology are used to design the optimization of cyber-based ecological learning environment, which can achieve its ecological balance, and help cultivate and maintain a healthy ecosystem of foreign language curriculum.

In 2004, "College English Curriculum Requirements" was issued by the Ministry of Education. Thereupon began a nationwide reform for college English teaching reform. After several years of practice, the Ministry of Education promulgated new "College English Curriculum Requirements" in 2007. Since the promulgation of the new Curriculum Requirements, the requirements for college English teaching reform are more comprehensive, and their objectives more clear. However, under the guidance of new systematic document, what is the application of modern information technology with cyber as the core to foreign language learning? The dissertation, first by reviewing and researching all unbalanced phenomenon in the environment of computers and networks from ecological viewpoint, and then conducting an empirical survey of optimizing the unbalanced learning environment, suggests that the construction and optimization should be based on theories of ecology, ecological balance and principles of ecology.

The integration of information technology into foreign language curriculum is actually a large ecosystem. Computer-network is just a linking point in the integrated ecosystem. Foreign language learners' ecological environment is a subsystem of the ecosystem, which is interdependent and mutually constrained with teaching ecological environment, etc., thus creating a larger compatible and dynamic ecosystem for foreign language learners. Therefore, from this regard, the optimization of cyber-based ecological learning environment for foreign language learners is an inseparable part of establishing and perfecting the entire ecosystem for foreign language curriculum.

7 Chapter

Conclusion

7.1

Research Review

Based on author's research work of individuals' ecological environment, this research is conducted through systematic and in-depth combing of relevant literature. It intends to deal with the imbalances brought about by the integration of information technology into foreign language teaching within foreign language learners' ecological environment.

Aiming at these problems, the research topic is finalized and the research idea is straightened out. Based on the topic-related literature reviews both domestic and abroad, theoretical framework of cyber-based ecological environment for foreign language learners can be established, under the guidance of which a relevant research can be launched and the research method can be secured.

The main research methodology in this study is based on the macro research method. With this macro research method, other research methods such as literature review, statistical analysis, case study, etc. are all adopted in order to prove the appropriateness and preciseness of some micro viewpoints and basic structures. The details are as follows. Five teachers from Qiongzhou University have conducted a series of experiments for the whole semester. 300 students were randomly chosen to do eight kinds of questionnaires, informal discussions and English tests, involving their experiences or viewpoints on the four sub-ecological environments（namely physical learning environment, resourceful learning environment, technological learning environment and emotional learning environment）, their actual use of computer networks in college English class, their perspective of teachers' role, students' role, and the positioning of computers, and the present situation of college students' autonomous English learning in the environment of networks and computers. With all of these, college students' actual needs and their opinions or suggestions are collected. This kind of analysis is to provide relevant empirical basis for building and optimizing the model of cyber-based foreign language learners' ecological environment.

On the basis of the theoretical framework and acquired empirical demonstrations, the pattern of cyber-based ecological learning and the model of cyber-based ecological environment for foreign language learners are to be constructed. The niche theory and the theory of ecological balance are especially used to optimize the four imbalanced sub-ecological environments. The fundamental requirements and principles for its optimization have been proposed. The four optimized ecological environments can essentially realize the informationization of foreign language as well as the foreinization of information technologies, that is to say, on one hand, the information technology can be maximumly integrated into foreign language curriculum to achieve the real application of computers and networks into students' learning and teachers' teaching; on the other hand, the information technologies are reflected by foreign language learning curriculum by cultivating students' interest in foreign language study and their language sense so that the students can readily handle all the problems in an informationized way during the process of foreign language learning. The four sub-ecological environments are of interdependence, interaction, mutual adaptation, and coordinative unification, constituting a wholly dynamic and balanced foreign language learners' ecological environment.

Finally, the limitations and deficient aspects of the study are listed, while prospects for a finer and more comprehensive ecological mode of foreign language education are proposed, offering some enlightening ideas for future study.

◆ 7.2 ◆

Innovations of the Study

7.2.1 Innovative Study of Optimizing Four Imbalanced Cyber-based Sub-environments

The ecological environment for foreign language learners under the background of computer networks can be summarized into the following four sub-environments: the physical environment, resourceful environment, technological environment and emotional environment, covering almost all the factors within foreign language learners' cyber-based ecological environment, such as foreign language learning mode, learning objective, learning concept, study method, means of study, learning materials, multimedia course system, learning conditions, the resources of teachers, the quality of students' enrollment, the necessary materials, learners' social environment, supervision mechanism, management level, emotional psychology, and so on. The integration of computer networks into foreign language teaching and learning has inevitably impacted on all the factors within the environment, which directly leads to the alternation of teaching and learning concept. All these changes are bound to break the ecological balance of traditional teaching environment. Consequently, the occurrence of all these imbalances has posed great challenges for traditional theories.

7.2.2 Innovative Study of Constructing an Optimized Ecological Environment Model for Cyber-based Sub-environments

Construct an optimized mode. The imbalanced cyber-based ecological environment for foreign language learners is optimized into an environment which not only can reflect ecological laws and principle, ready to be manipulated, perfected, optimized and developed, but also is a kind of student-centered integration of all ecological factors, casting a positive influence on learners.

The cyber-based ecological environment for foreign language learners is a sub-environment and subsystem of foreign language education system, in which the internal and external flows of materials, energy, information and emotion are continuously maintained with balanced total sum of inputs and outputs. The flow of these physical and natural substances in the flow of the main factors is to ensure that all infrastructures and teaching resources needed for regular leaning activities can be eliminated and updated timely and properly, which also includes the investment and flow of environmental hardware. For example, the investment in the construction of multi-media classrooms for learners is physical materials of cyber-based ecological learning environment input by foreign language education system. The energy flow in the cyber-based ecological learning environment mainly refers to the technical support provided by technological learning environment. Some of the energy is converted to three-dimensional learning materials while some part which is converted into multimedia technology is used to guarantee the normal operation of the cyber-based ecosystem. The flow of information certainly means the process of information transmission, processing, restructuring and decomposition by learners in resourceful learning environment. Within the cyber-based ecological learning environment, the information flow is in a dominant position, compared with the importance of material flow and energy flow. The shortage of energy flow and material flow will undoubtedly have a negative effect on the quality of constructing foreign language learning environment.

Lack of information flow will affect learners' updating of learning concept and renewal of learning content and learning styles. The smoothness of emotion flow is the internal factor which will have a huge impact on learners' learning efficiency. Sometimes, although there is big information flow and material flow within systems and environments, learners' learning quality will still be negatively influenced and the balance of learning eco-environment will still be broken if all flows move towards an incorrect direction.

The four sub-environments of physical learning environment, resourceful learning environment, technological learning environment and emotional learning environment are interdependent and mutually based. The balance of the entire cyber-based ecological learning environment depends on the balance of these four sub-environments and the fulfillment of function of subsystems. On the basis of these four sub-environments, various elements of the cyber-based learning environment are in interactive adaptations, and ultimately each element has found its proper and specific niche, that is, in good space-time positioning, maintaining the coherence and integrity of the overall function within the environment.

The focus of the whole optimization mode falls on foreign language learners. The core mechanism of ensuring the good functioning of foreign language learners' cyber-based eco-environment is to establish learner-centered learning mechanism. Through this mechanism, learners can carry out a variety of self-teaching forms such as supportive learning, service-based learning, instructive learning, stimulating learning, and evaluation-based learning within the cyber-based learning eco-environment, truly transforming the computers' status from "auxiliary" to "normalized" . The cyber-based ecological environment for foreign language learners, through the circulating operation of monitoring, regulation, improvement and optimization, will finally achieve foreign language learners' dynamic, healthy and sustainable development.

In a word, the integration of computer networks into foreign language curriculum forms learners' autonomous cyber-based learning environment. The purpose of constructing and optimizing this environment is for learners studying collaboratively via the network, free from spacetime and disciplines. The role of teachers is changed from learning guides to learning participators, together with learners to explore and gain knowledge. They share the learning tasks and resources in different groups. The lapped thoughts from them carry out two-way or multi-way interaction between learner-learner, learner-teacher and learner-computer. Learning extends from classroom to long distance, creating a harmonious learning environment. This is the second innovation of the current study.

7.3

Limitations of the Study

The present study of constructing an optimized foreign language learners' ecological environment under the background of multimedia networks, generally speaking, can be beneficial to the development of foreign language teaching practices. However, because of the author's limited knowledge, inadequate research ability, together with the restrictions of external environment, vigor and time, quite a number of problems do occur during the whole writing process.

First of all, the biggest problem of the study is the shortage of research materials. Materials on imbalances of learning environment are too few to be dug out, almost a blank in theoretical literatures of environmental optimization. It is difficult to collect resources on theoretical constructions relevant to the current study.

In addition, due to the complexity of the social science researches, there is no unity on the theories and standards of construction modes. Therefore, when it comes to choose related basis of model construction, it is an inevitable choice to take research theories, research methods and research objectives as the main basis according to the habitual criteria in the research work of social sciences, with literature resources, questionnaires and survey analysis being the complementary basis. Whether these conditions for mode construction are appropriate or not, it is of great necessity to consult experts.

Another limitation of the study is that the theory is inadequate because of the lack of theoretical literatures due to the author's insufficient study of relevant theory and insufficiency culture. In particular, the study of topic-based theories at home and abroad is far from enough and the understanding is far from in-depth. The study of theoretical generalization is neglected to some extent.

7.4

Future Prospects

This study is only targeting at the foreign language learners' ecological environment under the background of computer networks, and this environment is actually a sub-system of foreign language education system. So apart from the study on the integration of information technology into foreign language study within this system, it is hoped that future study can involve a higher level of integration which means the integration of construction factors like national education policy, foreign language disciplinary resources, academic resources, human resources and production resources. This kind of larger integration is conducted in an all-round way covering the links of management, disciplines, scientific research, human resources, production, etc., with the purpose of creating a more meticulous and overall mode for the construction and optimization of ecological environment.

The characteristics of foreign language education system have determined the exuberant vitality and bright prospects of this ecological environment. Along with the universal application of computer networks, the foreign language education system will attract more and more scholars to do researches owing to its striking features of ecology, openness and creation, technology and humanities. A more in-depth research can be conducted and it will become another important research area in the future study of foreign language learning.

Bibliography

English References

[1] Blake, R.J. New trends in using technology in the language curriculum [J] . *Annual Review of Applied Linguistics*, 2007 (27) : 76-97.

[2] Bowers, C.A. *Education, Cultural Myths, and the Ecological Crisis: Toward Deep Changes* [M] . Albany: State University of New York Press, 1993: 232.

[3] Bronfenbrenner, U. *The Ecology of Human Development: Experiments by Nature and Design* [M] . Cambridge, MA.: Harvard University Press, 1979: 330.

[4] Chapelle, C.A. Is networked-based learning CALL? [A] . *Network-Based Language Teaching: Concepts and Practice* [C] . New York: Cambridge University Press, 2000: 204-228.

[5] Cremin, L.A. Public education and the education of the public [J] . *Teachers College Record*, 1975 (77) : 1-12.

[6] Debski, R. Analysis of research in CALL (1980-2000) with a reflection on CALL as an academic discipline [J] . *ReCall*, 2003, 15 (2) : 177-188.

[7] Egbert, J. & G.M. Petrie. *CALL Research Perspectives* [M] . Mahwah, N.J.: Lawrence ErlbaumAssociates, 2005: 205.

[8] Farrell, T.S.C. Tailoring reflection to individual needs: a TESOL case study [J] . *Journal of Education for Teaching*, 2001, 27 (1) : 23-38.

[9] Gardner, H. *Frames of mind: the theory of multiple intelligence* [M] . New York: Basic Books, 1983: 530.

[10] Gardner, R.C. *Social Psychology and Second Language Learning: The Role of Attitudes and Motivation* [M] . London: Edward Arnold, 1985: 208.

[11] Goodlad, J.I. *Ecology of School Renewal* [M] . Illinois: University of Chicago Press, 1987: 235.

［12］John, E. *The Ecology of the School*［M］. London: Methuen, 1977: 127.

［13］Khan, B.H. Dimensions of E-Learning［J］, *Educational Technology*, 2002, 42（1）: 59-60.

［14］Leather, J. & J. Van Dam. *Ecology of Language Acquisition*［M］. Dordrecht: Kluwer Academic Publishers, 2003: 1-29.

［15］Levy, M. *Computer Assisted Language Learning: Context and Conceptualization*［M］. New York: Oxford University Press, 1997: 310.

［16］Levy, M. & D. Robert. *World CALL: global perspectives on computer-assisted language learning*［M］. Lisse: Swets & Zeitlinger.1999: 363.

［17］Levy, M. & F. Blin & C.B. Siskin, et al. *World CALL: international perspectives on computer-assisted language learning*［M］. London: Taylor & Francis, 2010: 115.

［18］Levy, M. & S. Glenn. *CALL Dimensions: options and issues in Computer-assisted language learning*［M］. New York: Routledge, 2006: 310.

［19］Philip, H. CALL and future teacher education［J］. *CALICO Journal*, 2008, 25（2）: 175-188.

［20］Tolboom, J. How to organize a digital learning environment: from technology to use ［Z］.Conference Paper ,Conference: Eunis, 2003:210.

［21］Tudor, I. *The Dynamics of the Language Classroom*［M］. Cambridge: Cambridge University Press, 2001: 244.

［22］Waller, W. *The Sociology of Teaching*［M］. New York: John Wiley, 1932: 467.

［23］Warschauer, M. Computer-assisted language learning: an introduction［A］. In S. Fotos （Eds.）. Multimedia Language Teaching［C］. Tokyo: Logos International, 1996: 3-20.

［24］Warschauer, M. & D. Healey. Computers and language learning: an overview［J］. *Language Teaching*, 1998 (31): 57-71.

［25］Zhao, Y. Language Learning on the World Wide Web: Toward a Framework of Network Based CALL.［J］. *The CALICO Journal*, 1996, 14(1): 37-51.

Chinese References—Articles

［1］安琦. 基于实证研究的网络语境下大学英语教学的生态化思考［J］. 外语电化教学，2009（3）: 58-62.

［2］陈坚林. 大学英语教学新模式下计算机网络与外语课程的有机整合——对计算机"辅助"外语教学概念的生态学考察［J］. 外语电化教学，2006（6）: 3-1.

［3］陈兴莉. 教育生态学视角下的大学英语教育改革［J］. 中国成人教育，2010（5）: 152-153.

［4］戴小华. 基于互联网的生态学交互式教学［J］. 赣南师范学院学报，2009（3）：
115-117.

［5］范国睿. 美英教育生态学研究述评［J］. 华东师范大学学报（教育科学版），1995
（2）：83-89.

［6］高凡，张媛媛. 构建大学英语网络自主学习与课堂教学整合的生态化模式［J］. 湖
北经济学院学报（人文社会科学版），2010（6）：199-200.

［7］顾曰国. 教育生态学模型与网络教育［J］. 外语电化教学，2005（4）：3-8.

［8］顾曰国. 教育生态学模型与网络教育［J］. 外语电化教学，2005：6.

［9］何高大. E-learning的定义与译名［J］. 中国科技翻译，2003（2）：62-63.

［10］贺祖斌. 高等教育生态研究述评［J］. 广西师范大学学报（哲学社会科学版），
2005：5.

［11］胡加圣. 基于范式转换的外语教育技术学学科构建研究［D］. 上海：上海外国语
大学，2012：225.

［12］黄若好. 对大学英语多媒体教学改革的探索［J］. 外语界，2000（1）：32-37.

［13］贺祖斌. 高等教育生态研究述评［J］. 广西师范大学学报（哲学社会科学版），
2005（1）：123-127.

［14］胡壮麟. 谈语言学研究的跨学科倾向［J］. 外语教学与研究，2007（6）：403-408.

［15］刘金侠. 网络教学环境中英语专业学生自主学习的探索［J］. 外语学刊，2009
（4）：119-122.

［16］刘森林. 生态化大学英语课堂模式设计研究［J］. 外语电化教学，2008（3）：
33-37.

［17］刘文宇，查吉安. 网络教学环境中英语学习者学习动机研究［J］. 外语学刊，2009
（3）：121-123.

［18］李荫华. 大学英语课程教学要求（试行）［J］. 中国大学教学，2004（1）：13-14.

［19］梅德明. 论系统外语教学［J］. 外语教学，1990（2）：12-14.

［20］莫锦国，汪玉霞. 沟通世界的桥梁——WorldCALL 2008国际研讨会评述［J］. 外
语电化教学，2009（4）：75-78.

［21］秦晨. 外语课堂的教育生态学解读［J］. 河海大学学报（哲学社会科学 版），
2005（3）：82-84.

［22］孙红. 构建学习者自主的语言学习环境［J］. 外语电化教学，2004（5）：64-67.

［23］孙秋丹，黄芳. 多媒体网络自主学习环境下大学英语四级成绩与学习策略的关系研
究［J］. 北京第二外国语学院学报，2010（2）：62-68.

［24］盛仁泽. 教育生态学视野中的大学英语多媒体课堂［J］. 长江师范学院学报，2008
（6）：140-143.

［25］宿晓华. 网络学习生态视角研究［D］. 山东：山东师范大学，2006：50.

［26］沈双一，陈春梅. "课堂教学生态系统"新概念刍议［J］. 历史教学问题，2004

（4）：92-95.

［27］谭玮. 论大学英语教学培养学习个性的教学原则［J］，外语学刊，2009（2）：131-133.

［28］谈言玲，等. 计算机辅助英语教学研究10年：回顾与思考［J］. 外语电化教学，2007（5）：37-42.

［29］魏晶，陈惠. 课堂环境的生态学思考［J］. 现代远距离教育，2008（2）：30-32.

［30］魏晶. 多媒体网络环境下外语学习者个体生态环境建构研究［J］. 外语电化教学，2010，（6）：69-76.

［31］王静. 美国网络学习环境的研究［D］. 上海：华东师范大学，2005：69.

［32］王立非. 外语教育：新世纪展望 新世纪外语教学研究的方法论展望［J］. 外语研究，2000（3）：9-10.

［33］王立非. 注意外语教学研究的方法论［J］. 外语与外语教学，1997（2）：20-22.

［34］吴启迪. 在大学英语教学改革试点工作视频会议上的讲话［Z］. 中国外语，2004，（1）：5.

［35］杨春慧. 试论多媒体计算机辅助英语教学的特点［J］. 外语电化教学，2000（1）：46-47.

［36］扬州. 多媒体在生态学教学中的积极作用［J］. 合肥师范学院学报，2004，22（3）：92-93.

［37］闫志明. 多媒体学习生成理论及其定律—对理查德.E.迈耶多媒体学习研究的综述［J］. 电化教育研究，2008（6）：11-15.

［38］张红玲，刘云波. 从网络外语教学研究现状看网络外语教学研究的学科框架［J］. 外语电化教学，2007（04）：8-13.

［39］张立新，李红梅. 虚拟学习环境的生态失衡及其对策探析［J］. 理论探讨，2009（7）：17-20.

［40］张立新，李世改. 生态化虚拟学习环境及其设计［J］. 中国电化教育，2008（6）：5-8.

［41］张立新，张丽霞. 虚拟学习环境的生态问题及其解决对策［J］. 电化教育研究，2010（10）：42-45.

［42］张丽霞，王文利. 生态系统视角下的虚拟学习环境的构建［J］. 中国电化教育，2010（8）：117-119.

［43］张肖莹，李天贤. 建构主义理论与多媒体机助大学英语教学［J］. 外语电化教学，2002（2）：22-26.

［44］周衍安，吴乃域. 课堂生态系统中师生角色探析——兼谈后现代主义的角色观［J］. 江苏大学学报，2003（4）：52-55.

［45］周衍安. 虚拟学习的生态观透视［J］. 现代远距离教育，2005，（6）：41-43.

［46］钟志贤. 论学习环境设计［J］. 电化教育研究，2005（7）：35-41.

Chinese References—Works

［1］程东元. 外语教学技术［M］. 北京：国防工业出版社，2008：235.

［2］陈洪，刘北利. 英语教育中的计算机应用［M］. 北京：人民教育出版社，2005：416.

［3］陈坚林，胡加圣. 信息技术与外语教学研究——理论构建与实践探索［M］. 上海：上海外语教育出版社，2010：349.

［4］陈坚林. 计算机网络与外语课程的整合——一项基于大学英语教学改革的研究［M］. 上海：上海外语教育出版社，2010：349.

［5］戴炜栋，胡文仲等. 中国外语教育发展战略论坛（1949-2009）［Z］. 上海：上海外语教育出版社，2009：925.

［6］戴正南，黄光远. 教育技术与外语教学［M］. 呼和浩特：内蒙古大学出版社，1988：161-162.

［7］方炳林. 生态环境与教育［M］. 台北：维新书局，1957：225.

［8］范国睿. 教育生态学［M］. 北京：人民教育出版社，2000：317.

［9］高等学校外语专业教学指导委员会. 大学英语教学大纲（修订本）［Z］. 1999.

［10］高等学校外语专业教学指导委员会英语组. 高等学校英语专业英语教学大纲［Z］. 北京：外语教学与研究出版社，2000：43.

［11］顾佩娅. 计算机辅助语言教学理论与实践［M］. 上海：复旦大学出版社，2006：340.

［12］顾曰国. 网络教育初探续集［C］. 北京：外语教学与研究出版社，2005：221.

［13］何高大. 现代教育技术与现代外语教学［M］. 南宁：广西教育出版社，2002：339.

［14］胡壮麟. 语言学教程［M］. 北京：北京大学出版社，2006：528.

［15］何兆熊，梅德明. 现代语言学 附现代语言学自学考试大纲［M］. 北京：外语教学与研究出版社，1999：379.

［16］贾国栋. 计算机辅助语言教学——理论与实践［M］. 北京：高等教育出版社，2007：224.

［17］刘日升，张泽梅. 信息技术与外语教学［M］. 大连：辽宁师范大学出版社，2007：282.

［18］李聪明. 教育生态学导论［M］. 台北：台湾学生书局，1989：165.

［19］梅德明. 现代语言学简明教程［M］. 上海：上海外语教育出版社，2003：309.

［20］梅德明. 新世纪英语教学理论与实践［M］. 上海：上海外语教育出版社，2004：578.

［21］任凯. 教育生态学［M］. 辽宁：人民辽宁教育出版社，1992：122.

［22］束定芳，庄智象. 现代外语教学——理论，实践与方法［M］. 上海：上海外语教育出版社，2004：263.

［23］文和平，杨晓莉，陈玖豪. 现代教育技术与外语教学实用教程［M］. 重庆：西南

师范大学出版社，2010：171.

［24］吴鼎福、诸文蔚.教育生态学［M］.南京：南京江苏教育出版社，1990：421.

［25］吴林富.教育生态管理［M］.天津：天津教育出版社，2006（6）：235.

［26］王立非、梁茂成.计算机辅助第二语言研究方法与应用［M］.北京：外语教学与研究出版社，2007：228.

［27］王琦.信息技术环境下的外语教学研究［M］.北京：中国社会科学出版社，2006：328.

［28］王守仁.高校大学外语教育发展报告（1978-2008)［Z］.上海：上海外语教育出版社，2008：293.

［29］雅各布，等.合作学习的教师指南［M］.北京：中国轻工业出版社，2005：180.

［30］闫寒冰.学习过程设计——信息技术与课程整合的视角［M］.北京：教育科学出版社，2005：251.

［31］曾方本.现代语言学理论与外语多媒体教学［M］.广州：暨南大学出版社，2010：273.

［32］张伯敏.现代信息技术环境下的外语教学［M］.海口：海南出版社，2006：256.

［33］张红玲，等.网络外语教学理论与设计［M］.上海：上海外语教育出版社，2010：579.

［34］中国社会科学院语言研究所词典编辑室.现代汉语词典［Z］.上海：商务印书馆，2005：1800.

［35］中华人民共和国教育部高等教育司编.大学英语课程教学要求［Z］.上海：上海外语教育出版社，2007：244.

［36］中华人民共和国教育部制订.英语课程标准（实验稿)［Z］.北京：北京师范大学出版社，2007：234.

Online Resources

1. http://xjjs.cbpt.cnki.net/WKC/WebPublication/index.aspx?mid=xjjs（现代教育技术）

2. http://news.163.com/11/0824/19/7C8DK8UO00014JB6.html（2011世界应用语言学大会暨第6届中国英语教学国际研讨会）

3. http://en.wikipedia.org/wiki/Alexander_von_Humboldt

4. http://en.wikipedia.org/wiki/Arthur_Tansley

5. http://en.wikipedia.org/wiki/August_Thienemann

6. http://en.wikipedia.org/wiki/Charles_Darwin

7. http://en.wikipedia.org/wiki/Haeckel

8. http://en.wikipedia.org/wiki/Karl_M%C3%B6bius

9. http://en.wikipedia.org/wiki/Robert_Boyle

10. http://en.wikipedia.org/wiki/English-language_learner
11. http://wenku.baidu.com/view/785eae6c58fafab069dc0247.html（Linderman）
12. http://shflet.com/news/INDEX.ASP.（上海市教育技术协会外语教育专业委员会年会）
13. http://www.china.com.cn/book/zhuanti/2008fy/node_7046396.htm.（2008第18届世界翻译大会）
14. http://www.chinalawedu.com/news/1200/22598/22615/22793/2006/3/he7396032197360029150-0.htm）（中共中央国务院关于深化教育改革全面推进素质教育的决定）
15. http://www.eltchina.org/2009beijing/.（中国教育学会外语教学专业委员会第15次学术年会）
16. http://www.flcetc.org（中国教育技术协会外语专业委员会网站）
17. http://www.gov.cn/zwgk/2007-05/23/content_623645.htm.（国务院批转教育部国家教育事业发展"十一五"规划纲要的通知）
18. http://www.meeting163.com/meeting/lw.asp?id=105.（第5届中国英语教学国际研讨会）
19. http://www.people.com.cn/item/flfgk/gwy/jkww/j940703.html.（国务院关于《中国教育改革和发展纲要》的实施意见）
20. www.china.com.cn（中国网：中华人民共和国教育部国家中长期教育改革和发展规划纲要2010-2020年）

附录1 关于"大学生物质学习环境情况"的调查问卷

各位同学：

您好！非常感谢您参与这次问卷调查！本问卷仅为了研究大学生外语学习情况，调查结果用于纯学术性研究性目的，不涉及个人隐私，请您耐心完成我们的设问，如有疑问，请联系我们的调查员。再次对您的参与表示感谢！

问卷说明：请根据自己的实际情况在"选项"这栏填上阿拉伯数字。（5分：完全符合；4分：50%以上符合；3分：50%符合；2分：50%以下符合；1分：基本不符合。）

学院：_____ 专业：_____ 年级：_____ 性别：_____

内　容	选　项
1. 您所在学校地处市中心	
2. 您所在校园周边有很多网吧、KTV等娱乐场所	
3. 您所在校园周边有很多餐馆、冷饮吧等美食场所	
4. 您所在校园周边有教育类书店	
5. 您所在校园周边有很多流动小商贩	
6. 您所在校区存在长期的施工建设现象	
7. 您所住宿舍周围是运动场	
8. 您的英语老师会经常使用多媒体语音教室授课	
9. 多媒体语音教室光线充足	
10. 在多媒体语音教室学习时，可以保证每人都有一台电脑	
11. 多媒体语音教室的电脑都配有耳麦和麦克风	
12. 多媒体语音教室的电脑坏了会有人及时来修理	
13. 英语老师知道如何操作多媒体语音教室的投影仪	
14. 投影仪的显示效果可以保证最后一排的同学都看得清屏幕	
15. 上课时，多媒体语音教室的计算机经常没有声音、死机甚至崩溃	
16. 您家里有电脑	
17. 您家的电脑只有在寒暑假才会联网	
18. 在家上网时，您的主要活动是看八卦新闻	

续表

内　　容	选　项
19. 在家上网时，您的主要活动是玩游戏	
20. 在家上网时，您的主要活动是聊天购物	
21. 在家上网时，您的主要活动是看美剧或电影	
22. 在家上网时，您的主要活动是听英文歌	
23. 在家上网时，您的主要活动是写博客	
24. 您有诸如快易典、文曲星等电子词典	
25. 您了解国家颁布的基于网络的多媒体立体化教学体系建设的政策	
26. 您学校对国家英语教学改革的政策落实到位	
27. 您学校支持学生使用计算机学习英语	
28. 您学校多媒体教室的管理有专人负责，而不是任课老师	

附录2 关于"大学生资源学习环境情况"的调查问卷

各位同学：

您好！非常感谢您参与这次问卷调查！本问卷仅为了研究大学生外语学习情况，调查结果用于纯学术性研究性目的，不涉及个人隐私，请您耐心完成我们的设问，如有疑问，请联系我们的调查员。再次对您的参与表示感谢！

问卷说明：请根据自己的实际情况在"选项"这栏填上阿拉伯数字。（5分：完全符合；4分：50%以上符合；3分：50%符合；2分：50%以下符合；1分：基本不符合。）

学院：_____ 专业：_____ 年级：_____ 性别：_____

内　容	选　项
1. 相比较多媒体授课，您依旧习惯于粉笔黑板的教学模式	
2. 您习惯边听老师讲课边做笔记	
3. 您能适应"小组讨论"等互动性教学活动	
4. 您能适应"启发提问"等探索性教学活动	
5. 您学英语是为了拿一个大学文凭	
6. 您想拿英语等级证书，因此花很多时间操练四六级考试题目	
7. 您觉得会英语的人才竞争力强	
8. 您对自己的英语学习已有规划	
9. 您有充分利用英语教材里的光盘	
10. 每一学期结束，您都完整地学习了整个英语教材	
11. 您觉得大学英语教材难度适中	
12. 您觉得网络版教材很个性化，并且简单实用	
13. 您能熟练运用外语学习中常用的计算机技术工具	
14. 您的英语老师经常使用多媒体教学	
15. 您觉得英语老师的课堂PPT很符合自己的学习特点	
16. 您发现英语老师制作的课件文字居多	
17. 您发现英语老师制作的课件图片居多	
18. 您觉得英语老师的多媒体课件内容适中	
19. 您觉得英语老师展示课件时间偏多	
20. 您觉得英语老师讲解课件时间偏多	

附录3 关于"大学生技术学习环境情况"的调查问卷

各位同学：

您好！非常感谢您参与这次问卷调查！本问卷仅为了研究大学生外语学习情况，调查结果用于纯学术性研究性目的，不涉及个人隐私，请您耐心完成我们的设问，如有疑问，请联系我们的调查员。再次对您的参与表示感谢！

问卷说明：请根据自己的实际情况在"选项"这栏填上阿拉伯数字。（5分：完全符合；4分：50%以上符合；3分：50%符合；2分：50%以下符合；1分：基本不符合。）

学院：_____ 专业：_____ 年级：_____ 性别：_____

内　容	选　项
1. 您觉得个性化学习模块真正的适合学生的发展	
2. 您觉得个性化学习模块的课程设置覆盖了不同专业	
3. 您觉得在计算机网络学习中，有小组讨论和协作学习模式	
4. 您觉得课堂信息过多，造成了无效信息泛滥	
5. 您觉得学校存在"无多媒体不成公开课"的现象	
6. 您觉得学校多媒体功能仅仅是作为投影仪在使用	
7. 在课堂提问中，老师喜欢套用"标准答案"	
8. 您觉得课件中的图片、声音和动画会分散注意力	
9. 您觉得老师的课件信息量适中	
10. 您觉得计算机学习平台可以实时监控上网聊天等现象	
11. 您觉得计算机学习平台能实时跟踪你的学习情况	
12. 您觉得利用计算机学习平台要花费更多的时间	
13. 您觉得教学信息量大，造成学生"迷航"	
14. 您知道如何处理"海量"的网络信息	
15. 您觉得计算机的滥用容易造成学生成绩不稳定	

附录4 关于"大学生情感学习环境情况"的调查问卷

各位同学：

您好！非常感谢您参与这次问卷调查！本问卷仅为了研究大学生外语学习情况，调查结果用于纯学术性研究性目的，不涉及个人隐私，请您耐心完成我们的设问，如有疑问，请联系我们的调查员。再次对您的参与表示感谢！

问卷说明：请根据自己的实际情况在"选项"这栏填上阿拉伯数字。（5分：完全符合；4分：50%以上符合；3分：50%符合；2分：50%以下符合；1分：基本不符合。）

学院：_____ 专业：_____ 年级：_____ 性别：_____

内　容	选　项
1. 您一天上网的时间超过2小时	
2. 您一天上网的时间少于1小时	
3. 您觉得自己能合理利用网络中的学习资源	
4. 您觉得自己能正确使用计算机学习平台	
5. 您觉得在多媒体环境下，独立自主的学习方式有利于学习成绩的提高	
6. 您觉得在多媒体环境下，有效的网络学习方法有利于学习成绩的提高	
7. 您觉得英语考试成绩会影响你的学习积极性	
8. 您觉得现在的大学生不会使用计算机是件很丢脸的事	
9. 您觉得经常使用多媒体进行英语学习影响视力	
10. 您觉得基于计算机平台的外语作业难度偏大	
11. 您觉得利用多媒体学习容易导致学习缺乏计划性和系统性	
12. 您觉得网络英语学习课业压力大	
13. 在多媒体教室学习时，如果遇到不会操作的问题，您会找同学或老师帮忙	
14. 利用计算机平台学习会减少您和同学合作交流的机会	
15. 您觉得在多媒体教室学习，不能及时地与其他同学进行参照比较	
16. 您觉得在多媒体环境下，有效的网络学习方法有利于学习成绩的提高	
17. 您觉得计算机网络与外语整合后的课堂老师仍有激情讲解	
18. 您觉得在多媒体教室学习，缺乏老师的直接关注	

续表

内　　容	选　项
19. 您觉得在多媒体教室学习，不能及时得到老师的反馈	
20. 您认同老师的多媒体教学理念	
21. 您觉得你与学习同伴之间的知识交流和共享很到位	
22. 您觉得你可以很好的使用各种网络工具和技术来存取学习材料、构建学习知识	
23. 您觉得对学习内容的理解透彻与否会影响你对新知识和旧知识的整合和构建	
24. 您觉得社会认可学生利用计算机网络进行英语学习	
25. 您觉得学校支持学生利用计算机网络进行英语学习	
26. 您相信利用计算机网络进行英语学习会有好的成绩	

附录5 关于"大学生英语课堂实际利用计算机网络的情况"的问卷调查

各位同学:

您好! 非常感谢您参与这次问卷调查! 本问卷仅为了研究大学生外语学习情况,调查结果用于纯学术性研究性目的,不涉及个人隐私,请您耐心完成我们的设问,如有疑问,请联系我们的调查员。再次对您的参与表示感谢!

学院:_____ 专业:_____ 年级:_____ 性别:_____

大学生英语课堂实际利用网络的情况	选　项
1. 您在实际的大学英语课堂中利用计算机网络进行学习吗? A.是,经常用; B.是,但只是偶尔用; C.不,几乎不用。	
2. 如果您现在正在利用计算机网络进行大学英语学习,您的主要活动是(可多选): A.看课件展示、听教师讲解,做笔记; B.词语操练、英汉翻译; C.参加课堂讨论、角色表演、情景对话等互动活动; D.集体协作共同完成学习任务; E.做大学英语四、六级模拟试题; F.不知道该做什么; G.其他_____。	
3. 您在实际的大学英语课堂中利用计算机网络进行学习时,遇到最大的技术问题是(可多选): A.文字处理; B.电子表格; C.数据库; D.网络浏览; E.多媒体演示; F.在线讨论工具的使用; G.其他_____。	
4. 在实际的大学英语课堂中利用计算机网络进行学习时,您认为教学软件存在的最大问题是(可多选): A.与实际教学需求存在一定的差距; B.信息超载或单一; C.多媒体素材只是简单罗列拼凑,缺乏系统性和科性; D.装饰性太强,过于花哨,学习主题不明确; E.交互性和兼容性很差,且不具有可编辑性; F.其他_____。	

续表

大学生英语课堂实际利用网络的情况	选　项
5. 实际的大学英语课堂中利用计算机网络进行学习时，您产生过一下哪种情绪（可多选）： A. 过度依赖或排斥网络； B. 由于不适应网络课程平台，产生厌学情绪； C. 新的学习模式带来的压迫感和焦虑感； D. 作业难度过大，有种挫败感； E. 作业难度过小，没有成就感； F. 担心视力下降； G. 其他＿＿＿＿＿＿＿＿＿＿＿。	

附录6 关于"学生对教师角色、学生角色和计算机角色的定位"的问卷调查

各位同学：

您好！非常感谢您参与这次问卷调查！本问卷仅为了研究大学生外语学习情况，调查结果用于纯学术性研究性目的，不涉及个人隐私，请您耐心完成我们的设问，如有疑问，请联系我们的调查员。再次对您的参与表示感谢！

问卷说明：请您根据自己的想法，并参照实际情况，对教师角色和学生角色分别进行重要性排序，阿拉伯数字1代表绝不重要，2代表基本上不重要，3代表偶尔重要，4代表基本重要，5代表非常重要。

学院：_____ 专业：_____ 年级：_____ 性别：_____

定位项		定位类型选项	排序
教学角色	课前	课程设计者	
		课程开发者	
	课中	课程讲授者	
		课程组织者	
		课程培训者	
		课程评价者	
	课后	课程协助者	
		学习资料提供者	
学生角色	课前	课程预习者	
		主动探索者	
	课中	积极提问者	
		协作学习者	
		被动接收者	
		课堂监控者	
	课后	教学评估者	
		学习资料融会贯通者	

续表

定位项	定位类型选项		排序
计算机角色	教师教学内容的演示工具		
	教学理念的具体展现工具		
	教师即时的评测反馈工具		
	师生之间的交流工具		
	个人自学的辅导工具		
	学习模式的启发工具		
	学习目标的实现工具		
	学生学习兴趣的激励工具		
	学生预习的准备工具		
	学生成绩的考核工具		

附录7 关于"在多媒体网络环境下，大学生自主学习英语的现状了解"的调查问卷

各位同学：

您好！非常感谢您参与这次问卷调查！本问卷仅为了研究大学生外语学习情况，调查结果用于纯学术性研究性目的，不涉及个人隐私，请您耐心完成我们的设问，如有疑问，请联系我们的调查员。再次对您的参与表示感谢！

问卷说明：请根据自己的实际情况在"选项"这栏填上阿拉伯数字。（5分：完全符合；4分：50%以上符合；3分：50%符合；2分：50%以下符合；1分：基本不符合。）

学院：_____ 专业：_____ 年级：_____ 性别：_____

内　容	选　项
1. 您选择校内住宿是因为校内环境有助于学习吗？	
2. 您觉得学校图书馆藏书丰富且安静吗？	
3. 您总能在图书馆找到自己心仪的图书吗？	
4. 您至少每周都要去一次图书馆借书或阅读吗？	
5. 您觉得学校教室光线充足吗？	
6. 您每天都会去教室上自习吗？	
7. 您每天自习时间都超过2小时吗？	
8. 您学校的宿舍有互联网端口吗？	
9. 您总能在互联网上搜索到想要的学习资源吗？	
10. 您知道大学英语课程所规定的课时数吗？	
11. 您知道总课时数中包括多少网络多媒体教学的课时数吗？	
12. 您知道大学英语老师授课一单元要花费几个课时数吗？	
13. 您知道大学英语课程的具体课程要求吗？	
14. 您知道大学英语教师每堂课要达到的教学目的吗？	
15. 您知道大学英语课程成绩评估方法吗？	
16. 您知道大学英语课程的考试题型吗？	
17. 在大学英语学习过程中，您给自己设定了学习目标吗？	

续表

内　容	选　项
18. 您觉得您可以达到自己所设定的学习目标吗？	
19. 为了实现英语学习目标，您是否制定了相应的学习计划？	
20. 在实施学习计划过程中，您觉得困难吗？	
21. 在实施学习计划过程中，您需要老师的指导吗？	
22. 在实施学习计划过程中，您需要同学的帮助和鼓励吗？	
23. 开学前，您会去书店买大学英语教材配的光盘吗？	
24. 课前，您会利用光盘、音频等音像制品进行预习吗？	
25. 预习过程中，您会把书本中有疑问的地方标记出来吗？	
26. 课前，您会利用互联网查找有关课题的资料吗？	
27. 课堂上，您会一边听老师讲授一边浏览PPT吗？	
28. 课堂上，您会参加英语情景对话或是模拟表演吗？	
29. 课堂上，您会与老师和同学一起讨论问题吗？	
30. 课后，您会经常拷贝教师的教学课件吗？	
31. 您喜欢老师的教学课件中图片、声音和动画等元素吗？	
32. 大学英语老师会通过网络课程、电子邮件等形式与您进行学习交流吗？	
33. 大学英语老师给您建议过英语学习方法吗？	
34. 大学英语老师会经常提醒您注意英语学习方法的使用吗？	
35. 您觉得这些方法对您的英语学习有效吗？	
36. 您会经常利用网络课程等平台来检测和记录自己的学习动态吗？	
37. 您是通过考试成绩来衡量学习方法的效度吗？	
38. 大学英语老师会经常布置作业吗？	
39. 大学英语老师会经常组织学生自学吗？	
40. 大学英语老师会随时反馈您的学习动态吗？	
41. 在利用网络课程平台学习大学英语时，您会跟其他学习者互相竞争吗？	

内　容	选　项
42. 在利用网络课程平台学习大学英语时，您会跟其他学习者分工合作吗？	
43. 在利用网络课程平台学习大学英语时，您会跟其他学习者进行角色扮演吗？	
44. 在利用网络课程平台学习大学英语时，您会跟其他学习者进行小组讨论吗？	
45. 您觉得自己充分意识到多媒体在外语学习中的重要性了吗？	
46. 您善于使用网络工具和技术存取学习材料吗？	
47. 您能将新知识和已学知识进行整合和重构吗？	
48. 您会跟身边的朋友介绍利用多媒体网络学习英语的情况吗？	
49. 您会跟家人交流利用多媒体网络学习英语的心得吗？	
50. 您自己会经常总结利用多媒体网络学习英语的成绩吗？	

附录8 计算机基本技能培训对学生利用多媒体参加听力考试成绩的影响

为了找出计算机基本技能培训是否会对学生利用多媒体平台参加听力考试成绩的提高产生影响，我们对琼州学院2009级甲班（共59人）进行了实验。首先，将甲班同学随机分为A、B平均两组；A组同学没有在多媒体教室进行计算机基本技能培训，而B组的同学有在多媒体教室进行计算机基本技能的培训。下面是两组同学分别的听力测试成绩。找出计算机操作能力培训是否会影响学生听力考试成绩的提高。

A组（30人）	B组（29人）
33.5	37.5
45	53
48	67
49	62
50.5	63
50.5	63
51	65
51.5	49.5
52	68
52.5	60
54	71
55.5	67.5
55.5	65
57	79
57.5	74
62.5	69
63.5	69.5
59.5	74
59.5	86
60	69

续表

A组（30人）	B组（29人）
63	76
67.5	75
64	72
65	87
66.5	75
66.5	83
66.5	81
69	75
70	86
78.5	

附录9 即时的反馈对错误的纠正的影响

　　人们常说，即时的反馈对错误的纠正很有效。然而，我们怀疑这种反馈会不会使学生更加紧张从而犯更多的错误呢？为了证明此，我们给出3种不同电脑测试，每一个测试都有2个部分。在做第一次测验时，我们坐在学生身旁，当其将要犯错时，我们立即阻止学生并且解释错误；在做第二次测验时，我们也坐在学生身旁，在他们犯错之后帮助其纠正错误。在做第三次测验时，我们让学生做完所有电脑测试组后，再告诉他们犯错的地方。每一个测验的第二部分都由学生独立完成。每篇练习中均有10处可能出错的地方。优秀的分数是0分，10分意味着学生在每处易出错处都错了。这些结果将用作研究数据。我们要检测这3个测试之间是否存在显著差异，如果存在，这些差异体现在哪里。

S	T1	T2	T3
1	2	6	4
2	4	6	2
3	3	9	6
4	1	2	3
5	3	1	2
6	6	9	3
7	9	8	7
8	1	3	2
9	3	1	2
10	4	2	3
11	2	3	1
12	2	3	1
13	3	2	1
14	2	3	1
15	5	5	2
16	3	2	1
17	6	4	2
18	2	3	1

附录10 综合英语的考试

实验1于2010年9月在琼州学院英语专业2009级中随机抽取一个班的30名学习者作为实验班。他们都来自海南省，学习英语的时间是7年，都通过高考入学考试，可以假设他们的英语水平一致。在这个基础上进行综合英语入学考试。实验2是同一个班每周在多媒体网络教室利用立体式教材进行4小时的综合英语学习，取其期末的综合英语的考试。

学生	学习前	学习后
1	65	76
2	73	74
3	88	92
4	81	88
5	86	79
6	59	63
7	95	95
8	75	84
9	82	85
10	69	74
11	66	78
12	87	90
13	85	91
14	76	80
15	68	77
16	80	85
17	58	66
18	79	87
19	64	56
20	75	83

续表

学生	学习前	学习后
21	84	89
22	72	78
23	81	96
24	77	89
25	80	88
26	72	85
27	68	75
28	83	91
29	75	82
30	63	77

附录11 对于外语课堂上的各种活动的作用性学生的意见

为了更好地指导外语教学，外语系要求学生对各种课堂活动的作用进行排序。外语系想知道是否学生的意见统一。新网络环境下的外语课堂活动有以下10项：（a）小组竞赛；（b）小组讨论；（c）写作文；（d）听力训练；（e）语法练习；（f）随堂测验；（g）问题解答；（h）词汇操练；（i）看英文电影；（j）情景剧模拟。以下是外语系调查员收集的数据。

零假设：对于外语课堂上的各种活动的作用性，学生不持一致意见。

S	a	b	c	d	e	f	g	h	i	j
1	9	10	6	1	7	8	2	4	3	5
2	10	9	7	2	6	8	3	5	4	1
3	9	8	6	1	5	10	4	3	2	7
4	4	9	6	8	10	3	7	2	5	1
5	10	9	6	1	7	8	3	5	2	4
6	9	10	6	1	7	8	3	5	2	4
7	6	7	1	4	9	2	10	5	8	3
8	10	9	7	2	5	8	3	6	4	1
9	9	10	6	1	8	7	3	5	1	4
10	8	6	2	5	10	9	7	4	3	1
11	9	8	6	1	5	10	4	3	2	7
12	9	10	6	1	7	8	4	5	3	2
13	1	6	7	10	9	8	2	4	3	5
14	9	10	6	1	8	7	3	5	2	4
15	6	3	10	8	1	2	5	4	7	9